English Pottery and Porcelain Marks

Stanley W. Fisher, F.R.S.A.

Member of the British Antique Dealers' Association Limited

W. Foulsham & Co. Ltd
Yeovil Road, Slough, Bucks, England
LONDON · NEW YORK · TORONTO · SYDNEY · CAPE TOWN

W. Foulsham & Co. Ltd
Yeovil Road, Slough, Bucks, England

By the same author
English Blue and White Porcelain of the 18th Century
The Decoration of English Porcelain
China Collector's Guide
Collector's Progress
British Pottery and Porcelain
English Ceramics
Worcester Porcelain

ISBN 0-572-00711-6

Filmset by Keyspools Ltd, Golborne, Lancashire
Printed and bound in Great Britain by
Tinling (1973) Ltd, Prescot, Merseyside

Contents

Introduction

My intention in compiling this little book is to make available reproductions of the commoner marks to be found on British Pottery and Porcelain between *c.* 1750 and the beginning of the twentieth century. Also to provide a necessarily limited amount of useful information concerning the wares themselves.

Later marks are omitted as being self-explanatory, as are many factory marks which were used on some particular, usually printed design. Similarly, it has been necessary to omit what are usually known as 'workmens' marks', the kind often found for example on early blue painted Worcester porcelain and used to indicate the work of a particular decorator or batch of wares.

Before confirming the identification of a piece through its mark, one must be able to recognise that it is of a particular kind of ware and the several types are classified as follows:

Porcelain

A translucent ware, usually white in colour and either 'hard paste' or 'soft paste'. Hard paste is made of China Clay and China Stone in the Oriental or more usually Continental manner and is fired at a very high temperature.

Soft paste, with few exceptions, is made in the English manner with an additional mixture of bone ash, steatite clay or some other substance and is fired at a lower temperature.

In general, there is no rule-of-thumb method by which the beginner can distinguish between these two kinds of paste. There are important differences in their textures and usually, though not always, in their appearance. The enamels do tend to 'take' differently on their surfaces, but ready recognition can only be the result of experience gained through handling specimens of each kind.

Earthenware

Opaque and of any colour; made of some kind of clay.

Stoneware

An earthenware, vitrified at a high temperature and often semi-translucent in its thinner parts.

In addition to the differing types of ceramics, there are various kinds of protective glaze to be found on them. One finds a fine white glaze on delft which effectively covers the coloured clay beneath. An ordinarily clear, colourless, lead glaze and on a class of eighteenth ware known as 'Salt-glazed' a typical pitted surface like an orange. In addition to colourless lead glazes there are some to which colour has been added.

Impressed Marks

Which are stamped into the body of the soft-unfired clay and are well-nigh impossible to 'fake'.

Raised Marks

Which their name implies, stand above the surface as in the case of the early Chelsea 'Raised Anchor' applied in the form of a tiny pad of clay.

Incised Marks

Which are similar to Impressed Marks except that though they are applied to the soft unfired clay in the same way, they are scratched in, not stamped upon.

Underglaze in Blue

Which were printed or painted by hand onto the surface of the ware before the glaze was applied.

Overglaze Marks

Which were of any colour, and were printed or painted onto the surface of the ware after the glaze had been fired. A comparatively low temperature was needed to fire them and for this reason they are the easiest to 'fake'.

Apart from the marks which were invented by manufacturers to enable their wares to be recognised, many were copied from foreign originals, usually when the intention was to imitate or rival a particular style of Oriental or Continental decoration. Thus, Worcester copies of Meissen carry the borrowed 'crossed swords' mark and pseudo Chinese numerals were applied to wares decorated in the 'Japan' style. And at Coalport pieces decorated in the French manner were occassionally marked with the 'hunting horn' of Chantilly. Moreover, when the little Lowestoft factory tried to rival Worcester porcelain decorated in underglaze blue they often borrowed that factory's open crescent and at secondhand, its Meissen crossed swords. These are only some examples of what was very common practice in the early years.

It should be stressed that a mark is but a final clinching proof of provenance after considerations of paste, potting, glaze and decoration have already led to a definite conclusion. Many early factories were haphazard in their use of marks and even at a later period, as in the case of Chamberlains at Worcester it was common to mark only one piece of a service. It is important also to understand that a tea-service for example, was not made as a unit. Cups, saucers, and other items were made in batches, stored, and taken from the shelves as required. The result is that many a cup and saucer of early Worcester, for instance, may not only show different translucencies (the result of slightly different mixes of ingredients) but also different marks (such as a crescent and a 'fretted square' respectively).

Finally, as most beginners know to their cost, a mark may deceive. Thus, when during the second half of the 19th century Samson of Paris made his technically perfect 'Reproductions of Ancient Works emanating from the Museums and from private collections' he applied the Chelsea *gold anchor*, the Derby *crossed batons*, *Crown and D*, and the Worcester *fretted square*, to his 'hard paste' copies of the English 'soft paste' originals. Fortunately, if a specimen of the genuine and one of the imitation are studied side-by-side the difference between the marks, to say nothing of the paste, glaze and decoration, will prevent any future mistake.

Finally, it must be clear that a piece of pottery or porcelain may often be approximately dated by its mark. Worcester 'workmen's marks' for example were used only during a limited early period; pattern marks including the pattern name, were only used after about 1810, and any mark incorporating the Royal Arms or the word *Royal* is of the nineteenth century or later. The word 'England' appears in marks used from 1891, and 'Made in England' is proof of twentieth century origin.

Pictorial Glossary

Agate Ware

Produced by a very specialised technique, the ware is usually associated with figures made by Astbury and table ware made by Whieldon between *c.* 1740 and 1750. At best, Whieldon's ware was made in solid agate, as the tankard here illustrated. Pieces were made by layering clays of different colour, doubling and slicing. Later wares were given a surface agate effect by painting, combing or mingling together several colours of slip (liquid clay) onto an ordinary clay body. This later process was used in the 1770's and 1780's by Wedgwood and Bentley in the making of a wide range of marbled effects.

Whieldon tankard, 6″ high, *c.* 1740–50

Belleek

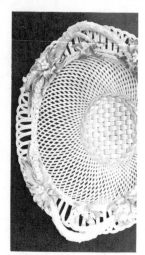

The best known of the ware associated with the Irish pottery in County Fermanagh is that which was fashioned in traditional marine shapes. A speciality, however, was open-work baskets of the kind illustrated whose form was probably introduced by Staffordshire workmen familiar with creamware shapes. The mark upon this example is the standard printed mark of tower, dog and harp. It should be noted that this pottery is still in production, and many of the patterns of the early period are still made.

Basket, 11″ long, *c.* 1860–70

Derby group, *c.* 1795

Biscuit

Biscuit or bisque porcelain is a once-fired body without glaze. It is particularly suitable for figure making, since detail is not in any way obscured. Popular on the continent and in this country in the 18th century, it was used at Derby from about 1770 onwards. The best modeller was John James Spengler (or Spangler, son of the Director of the Zurich porcelain factory.) who was at Derby *c.* 1790–1800. Biscuit figures were made during the early 19th century at several other factories, notably at Mintons. In *c.* 1846 a new body called 'Parian' was invented by Copelands while attempting to find the secret of Derby biscuit. Parian was used thereafter in preference to ordinary biscuit because of its creamier colour.

Wedgwood group, 19″ high, *c.* 1770–80

Black Basalt

Basalt or 'Egyptian Black' was used at many factories for the making of tea wares from about 1760, and in a much improved form by Josiah Wedgwood from *c.* 1773 to make classical figures, vases, plaques, etc. The improved stoneware body was smoother and a deeper black than that used, for example, by the Elers and Twyford. And it was ideally suited to fine modelling and engine turning. Wedgwood used it not only in its plain black form but also decorated it with unglazed enamels, relief ornamentation in red, and occasionally simulated the appearance of bronze by adding metalic powder to the mix. This 'Faun and Bacchus' is a good example of this kind of ware.

Worcester plate, 7" diam., *c.* 1765–70

Blue and White

Much of our earliest 18th century porcelain was decorated in underglaze cobalt blue, to imitate and rival the 'Blue Nankin' imported from China. At first the decoration, usually in pseudo-Chinese style, was painted, but by *c.* 1765 the process of overglaze printing, invented simultaneously it would seem at Worcester and Liverpool, had been adapted to underglaze blue use. Much of this printed ware was made at Worcester, Caughley, Liverpool, Lowestoft and other factories. This plate, marked with the hatched crescent, is printed in the centre with the familiar 'pine-cone' pattern, while the border is painted. The appearance of this early blue and white is entirely different from that of the abundant blue-printed domestic wares made at Spodes and elsewhere during the period *c.* 1780–1840.

Leeds cruet, *c.* 1780

Creamware

Creamware was made as early as *c.* 1720, when Astbury added white clay and flint to his bodies. By about 1750 it was widely produced throughout the Potteries, as being a vast improvement on any other cheaply produced domestic ware and indeed a dangerous rival to porcelain. Though its ultimate development was due to Wedgwood, who by 1767 had surpassed all his rivals in this sphere, Leeds creamware, made under the proprietorship of Hartley, Greens & Co, was also very fine between *c.* 1780 and 1800. The piece illustrated is typical of the perforated ware which was made, each opening, like the Oriental 'rice-grain' porcelain, being made with a separate punch and not, as was later done at Wedgwoods, by a multiple tool.

Delft

Delft has a light, porous body covered with an opaque, white oxide-of-tin glaze upon which decoration may be painted in blue or polychrome. Its name is taken from the Dutch town of Delft, because its manufacture reached England from the Netherlands in the 16th century. In due course this settled into three main centres — London, Bristol and Liverpool. Most early Delft was decorated in Chinese styles, in a dashing, often crude manner which was enforced by the absorbent nature of the glaze. Because the ware had comparatively little strength and, as may be seen in this illustration, the glaze was apt to chip easily, it was dropped for the making of domestic wares in favour of the cleaner, lighter, durable creamware.

Lambeth posset-pot, *c.* 1700

Doulton Ware

The decorative stoneware made at Doulton's Art Pottery from 1871 onwards is notable for its fine design and the accomplished decoration for which students from the Lambeth School of Art were responsible. Each example bears the mark of the decorator as well as the factory mark and often the date of manufacture. Thus, from L. to R. the illustration shows light blue slip decoration on a white body by Hannah B. Barlow, 1876, incised decoration filled in with cobalt blue on a white slip background by the same artist, 1875, and carved decoration with light blue and brown colouring by Arthur B. Barlow, 1873.

Various Doulton styles, 1873, 75 and 76

13

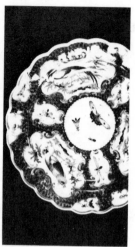

Worcester plate, 7¾″ diam., *c.* 1768–76

Exotic Birds

The so-called 'exotic birds' which are to be seen on many early English porcelains had their origin in the 'fantasie-vögell' invented in the 1770's at Meissen, and Worcester in particular. The painting of these incredible yet colourfully decorative creatures was developed to a remarkable extent. They were used in many different kinds of design, and are to be found in many distinctive styles, some being painted by London decorators and some by factory artists. The plate illustrated here, bearing the 'fretted square' mark, shews the characteristic Worcester combination of a scale-blue ground, upon which are gilt-scrolled reserves of birds and insects. It should be noted that this particular decorative style was often copied by Samson of Paris.

Vase, 1887

Martin Ware

The Martin brothers were early representatives of what we now call 'Studio Potters' – others were Bernard Moore and William de Morgan – who produced salt-glazed stonewares of outstanding quality first at Fulham and then later at Southall. One of the brothers, Walter, was trained at Doultons' pottery at Lambeth, and indeed there is a strong similarity between the wares made at Lambeth and those made by the Martins. Their pottery is best known for the much prized jugs in the forms of grotesque, almost horrifying animals and birds. The vase illustrated, bearing an incised pattern of fish and sea plants on a fawn ground, is representative of the more restrained kind of Martin ware, and bears the full incised, written mark together with the numerals 8–87.

Mason's Ironstone China

A very strong earthenware, patented by Charles James Mason in 1813, to meet the demand for showy, often gaudy ware by those who could not afford fine porcelain. Of this new body Mason made a wide range of dinner and dessert services, vases, jugs, and even fireplaces.

The Chinese influence is usually present both in design and decoration. The Chinese landscapes of the pieces illustrated have transferred pink outline washed in with enamels, and while the vases are heavily gilded, the jug, instead, has yellow enamel instead of the gold, a common Mason practice. It should be noted that a striking variety of the ware has fine gilding, or gilding and thick enamels applied upon a rich mazarine-blue ground, and that occasionally a piece may be found bearing panels of fine painting of landscape, flowers or fruit.

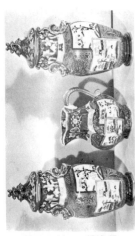

Vases and jug, *c.* 1813–25

Moulded Ware

Liverpool tea-pot, 8" high, *c.* 1750–70

Since so much pottery and porcelain was made in moulds, skilled modellers could not only fashion their own original designs, but were able at will to copy silver shapes and the designs used at other factories. While some early factories, such as Worcester, made great use of moulded forms from the beginning, others such as New Hall confine their attention to shape alone, with no attempt at decorative detail. Once thought to have been made at Longton Hall, the type of tea-pot illustrated here, with its crisp moulding of palm-trees and strawberry-leaves, has now been credited to Liverpool.

Oriental Decoration

When European potters began to decorate on porcelain they were obliged to rely upon Oriental sources for their designs — they were venturing into unknown territory, with no past experience. Most styles were imitations of the Chinese, often but not always Anglicised. Use was also made of the often simpler designs, mainly in red, blue, green and gold, of the Japanese potter Kakiemon. Bow porcelain in particular was so decorated, but this fine Worcester vase, marked with an open crescent and made *c.* 1770, is painted with what Worcester called the old pheasant Japan pattern' reserved on a scale-blue ground, with the usual scrolling in fine honey gold.

Worcester vase and cover, *c.* 1770

Powdered Blue

Amongst all the types of painting in underglaze blue on 18th century English porcelain, powdered blue is particularly attractive. This ground colour, copied from the Chinese, was applied by blowing the dry pigment through a tube, closed at one end with gauze, over the moistened surface of the ware, thus giving the granulated appearance visible in the photograph. The reserves were of course masked during the process. The central reserve contains an exceedingly rare subject, in that the name of the factory responsible for its manufacture, Bow, is to be seen written on the base of the vase. It may be dated *c.* 1755–60. Powdered blue was also used at Worcester, Caughley and Lowestoft.

'Bow plate, *c.* 1755–60

Pratt Ware

Bread plate dated 1851.

The name of F. & R. Pratt of Fenton is associated with a new way of printing in multicolours, each applied from a separate plate. This is seen not only on their well-known pot-lids but also upon dessert services, tea-wares, mugs, jugs, etc. This kind of ware was shown at the 1851 Exhibition, for which event this bread plate was specially produced by Jesse Austin, the chief designer, after H. Warren's 'Christ in the Corn-field'.

Pratt Ware

Jug, 8" high, *c.* 1820

Another kind of popular Pratt Ware takes the form of moulded jugs, such as this 'Parson and Clerk', made between *c.* 1780 and 1800 by William Pratt of Lane Delph, father of Felix and Richard. The mark PRATT is sometimes found impressed, but similar jugs were made elsewhere. The high temperature fired coloured glazes Pratt used are quite distinctive.

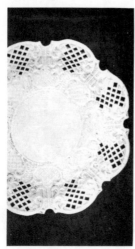

Staffordshire dish, *c.* 1750–60

Salt-glazed Ware

By about 1720 Staffordshire potters had evolved a pottery which by reason of its lightness, thinness, durability and delicacy was a fair substitute for imported Chinese porcelain. This was a white stoneware, high fired so as to become semi-vitreous, and glazed with salt thrown into the kiln at a temperature above 2,000 degrees F. to combine chemically with the silicate in the clays to form a durable sodium silicate glaze which has a characteristic, pitted appearance like orange-skin. At a later date, after about 1740, the ware was often gaily enamelled, but plain white moulded examples such as this are most attractive.

Slipware

Pilgrim flask, mid-14th century

Slipware is the earliest kind of earthenware which can be considered to be characteristically English. It is so called because a creamy mixture of clay and water, called 'slip', was used for its decoration. Slip was either painted on in large areas, trailed in lines and dots from a quill-spouted pot, or 'combed' into the surface of the ware. Alternatively, as in this example, it was used sparingly and thinly to impart colour interest. The piece illustrated is a rare Pilgrim Bottle dating from about 1350, lead-glazed, with splashes of white slip and applied foliate ornamentation.

Stone China

Stone china, as pioneered by Josiah Spode the Second, was the precursor of Mason's Ironstone China, being first produced in 1805 and quickly copied throughout the Potteries, under various names. Although of hard, clean appearance it is, of course, an earthenware whose smooth surface has been whitened by blueing. Spodes decorated with transferred patterns mostly in the Chinese style, though often translated into the English idiom. The outline was always printed in a colour suited to the washed-in enamels, in this case in sepia.

Spode plate, c. 1810–20

Stoneware

Compared with white salt-glazed stoneware, specimens of this kind, which was made at Fulham about 1760, may appear clumsy in the extreme. They comprise however an important class of English earthenware which was made in London, Nottingham and elsewhere from the 17th century onwards. The applied ornamentation suggests that the piece chosen for illustration was made for a bell-ringer whose initials B.H. it bears. As is usual with this kind of tankard the colour ranges from brown to buff, and the characteristic 'orange-skin' pitting of the salt glaze is clearly visible.

Fulham tankard, 8″ high, c. 1760

Porcelain Marks

Belleek Pottery
Belleek, Co. Fermanagh, Ireland. Founded 1863.
1. Impressed or printed, 1863–80.
2. Impressed or printed, the standard mark 1863–91. Continued in various forms. 'Co. Fermanagh' and 'Ireland' added *c.* 1891.

Distinguished by a nacreous glaze often contrasted with the unglazed parts of the Parian style body. Tea-wares (very thinly potted). Dessert and cabaret sets, figures, and ornamental wares often modelled after marine motifs. Great use of delicate shading in green or pink.

Bow China Works
Stratford, London. c. 1747–c. 1776.
1 & 2. Early incised marks.
3. Anchor and dagger mark, painted, *c.* 1760–76.
4. In underglaze blue, *c.* 1760–76.
5 & 6. Impressed marks of the 'repairer' Tebo, but also found on other porcelains.

Usually sensible durable wares, in contrast with those made at Chelsea, which catered for a more fashionable clientele. Much painted underglaze blue decoration and use of Japanese Kakiemon designs and of the famille-rose enamels of pink, pale green, pale opaque blue and aubergine (purplish mauve). Good figures, at first crude and heavy, but neater after *c.* 1754, when scrolled bases replaced plain ones.

Bristol ('hard paste' factory)
*Founded by William Cookworthy c. 1770, later Cook-
worthy and Richard Champion, closed 1781.*
These painted marks are found in many forms, with
different painters' numbers.

In common with Plymouth and New Hall they were makers of true porcelain,
resembling white glass, with a thin, colourless glaze and a pale grey trans-
lucency. Often recognisable by 'wreathing' (the marks of the potter's fingers
as he worked at his wheel) inside bowls, jugs, mugs, etc.

Caughley (or Salopian) Works
*Nr. Broseley, Shropshire. Proprietor Thomas Turner, and
later John Rose & Co. 1775–99.*
1–3. Printed in underglaze blue on underglaze blue
wares *c.* 1775–90.
4. Printed in underglaze blue on underglaze blue
wares *c.* 1775–90, and not to be confused with the
Worcester crescent.
5. Painted in underglaze blue on powder-blue
wares *c.* 1775–90.
6 & 7. Impressed, usually in lower-case letters *c.*
1775–90, and sometimes accompanied by underglaze
blue marks.

Pronounced CALFLEY, and until recently regarded as makers of rather inferior
ware in the Worcester style. There has now been a wide reclassification of
much of the porcelain made at the two factories, in the light of recent site
excavations.

Chelsea Porcelain Works

Chelsea, London. c. 1745–69.

1 & 2. Incised *c.* 1745–50. Rarely with the year 1745.

3. The 'raised anchor' mark on a raised pad of clay *c.* 1749–52. The anchor sometimes in red.

4. Small red anchor of the 'red anchor' period *c.* 1752–6.

5. Rare early mark in underglaze blue *c.* 1748–50.

6 & 7. Anchor in gold of the 'gold anchor' period *c.* 1756–59, and sometimes found on Derby wares painted at Chelsea *c.* 1769–75.

N.B. A large blue anchor is very occasionally found on pieces painted in underglaze blue.

In its day, the English rival of Meissen and other Continental factories in the production of elegant porcelain. Fine figures made from an early date, often lovelier than the Continental originals from which they were copied, but in turn much imitated by Samson of Paris, whose versions usually bear gold anchor marks.

Chelsea-Derby

William Duesbury of Derby purchased the Chelsea factory in 1769, and porcelains were decorated at Chelsea until c. 1784.

1. In gold, and rarely in red.

2 & 3. In gold.

Coalport Porcelain Works

Coalport, Shropshire, proprietors John Rose & Co., c. 1795, and at Stoke-on-Trent c. 1926 onwards.

1–4.   Painted in underglaze blue on all kinds of ware, *c.* 1810–25.

5.   Impressed mark on flat wares *c.* 1815–25.

6.   The Meissen 'crossed swords' in underglaze blue *c.* 1810–25. Note that the same mark is found on Worcester and Lowestoft porcelains.

7.   In enamels or in gold *c.* 1851–61.

8.   In enamels or in gold *c.* 1861–75, the letters denoting Coalport, Swansea and Nantgarw. John Rose had purchased the stock, moulds etc. of the Welsh factories *c.* 1820–22.

9.   An early painted mark, also found in circular form, *c.* 1805–15. Specimens may be seen in the Godden and V. & A. Collections.

10.   The crown mark *c.* 1881 onwards. 'England' was added *c.* 1891, and 'Made in England' from *c.* 1920. The date refers to the founding of the original earthenware manufactory at Caughley.

N.B. The names 'Coalport' and 'Coalbrookdale' are synonymous, and do not indicate that there were two factories.

Always of excellent quality, particularly after the purchase of the moulds and stock-in-trade of the Welsh factories, and the employment of Billingsley. Most early wares were unmarked, but the names and work of many of its Victorian artists, *c.* 1840–80, are known.

Derby Porcelain Works

The original works, founded c. 1750, closed in 1848, and a new one was started in King Street by former employees whose names appear in the marks used – Locker & Co., Courtney, and Stevenson Sharp, c. 1849–63. The factory was taken over by Stevenson & Hancock c. 1859. The marks of the modern Royal Crown Derby Porcelain Company Ltd., est. 1876 are self-explanatory.

1. Incised *c.* 1770–80, also occasionally in blue.
2. Painted *c.* 1770–82.
3. Standard painted mark, in puce, blue or black *c.* 1782–1800, and in red *c.* 1800–25.
4. Rare painted mark *c.* 1795.
5. Printed mark of the Bloor period *c.* 1825–40.
6. Printed mark of the Bloor period *c.* 1820–40.
7. Printed mark of the Bloor period *c.* 1830–48.
8. Painted mark of Stevenson & Hancock *c.* 1861–1935.
9. Printed mark of the modern company *c.* 1878–90.
N.B. The standard mark *c.* 1890 onwards is an elaboration of No. 9, with the words 'Royal Crown Derby' above the crown, 'England' or, after *c.* 1920, 'Made in England'.

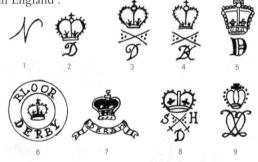

The products of the Derby factories span the history of porcelain-making from *c.* 1750 to the present day, and in addition to the decorative styles peculiar to Derby, almost every type of decoration was attempted, especially under Duesbury, with an eye to commercial success. When the Chelsea, Bow and Longton Hall concerns were taken over, the manufacture of many of their characteristic styles was continued. No contemporary factory employed a larger or more expert staff of specialist painters, who decorated not only everyday wares, but the beautiful cabinet specimens for which Duesbury's factory is famous.

Liverpool

The wares of many 18th century potteries have not yet been fully classified, and are rarely marked, with the exception of porcelain made at the Herculaneum Pottery, c. 1793–1841.

1 & 2. Painted in enamels or in gold, probably by Seth or James Pennington *c.* 1760–80.

3. Painted, and probably a Pennington mark *c.* 1760–80.

4 & 5. Impressed or printed *c.* 1796–1833.

6. Impressed or printed *c.* 1833–6. The 'Liver Bird' mark is found in many forms.

7. Impressed or printed *c.* 1796–1833.

N.B. The full name of the factory – 'Herculaneum Pottery' – was probably used, impressed, from about 1822.

It should be remembered that because a Worcester potter named Podmore went to Liverpool to join Richard Chaffers in 1755, to introduce the kind of steatite porcelain made at Worcester, there is often a marked similarity between some Liverpool and Worcester of the 'blue and white' variety.

Longton Hall Works

Founded by William Littler at Longton Hall, Stafford-shire; c. 1749–60.

Few pieces are marked, but the marks illustrated are occasionally found on early wares painted in under-glaze blue.

It is interesting to reflect that as far as we know, this was the only porcelain-making factory in the great potting centre of Staffordshire. Littler is best known as the inventor of the distinctive, vivid ground colour called 'Littler's Blue', which he first used upon earthenware before venturing into porcelain making.

27

Lowestoft Porcelain Works

Lowestoft, Suffolk, c. 1757–1802.

1 & 2.   Copies of the Worcester crescent and Meissen crossed swords marks, in underglaze blue, on blue-and-white wares, *c.* 1775–90.

3–5.   Examples of artists' marks, in underglaze blue, on blue-and-white wares *c.* 1760–75, usually painted near or inside the foot-rim.

1	2	3	4	5

This small factory made mostly domestic wares, often of toy-like quality, simply decorated in underglaze-blue painting or printing, or enamelled. At risk of repetition, it must be stressed that the factory was not responsible for the so-called 'Chinese Lowestoft' which was made in China for export to Europe. A great deal of ware has underglaze-blue patterns similar to those used at Worcester and Caughley, and is often marked with the Worcester crescent or crossed swords.

Lund's Bristol

('soft paste' factory)

Redcliff Backs factory c. 1748–51, owned by Benjamin Lund, and taken over by the Worcester proprietors.

The mark illustrated, in relief, is very rarely found upon moulded wares, and may be coupled with the equally rare relief mark WIGORNIA on cream-jugs and sauce-boats made at the Worcester factory at the time of the take-over.

BRISTOL

Not to be confused with the 'hard paste' factory. It is most difficult to distinguish between Lund's Bristol (sometimes referred to as 'Redcliffe Backs') and very early Worcester, though the typical enamelled decoration found on some of it, of Oriental derivation, is recognisable by its jewel-like, dainty quality.

Minton

Stoke-on-Trent, Staffordshire, Est. 1793.

1. Painted mark on porcelains made *c.* 1800–30, with or without a pattern number below.
2. Incised or impressed on early Parian figures *c.* 1845–50, sometimes with the year cypher.
3 & 4. Examples of printed marks indicating the several partnerships, e.g. Minton *c.* 1822–36, Minton & Boyle 1836–41, Minton & Co. 1841–73, and Minton & Hollins *c.* 1845–78. C.f. Nos. 6–8.
5. The 'ermine' mark, painted, from *c.* 1850 onwards, with or without the letter M.
6–8. Examples of the numerous printed marks which incorporate an indication of the partnership (and period) and, sometimes, a pattern name.
9 & 10. Printed marks of the 1860's.
11. Standard printed 'globe' mark *c.* 1863–72. A crown was added *c.* 1873, and an S to the word MINTON. In 1891 'England' was added below, and 'Made in England' *c.* 1902. See Year Cyphers, p. 69.

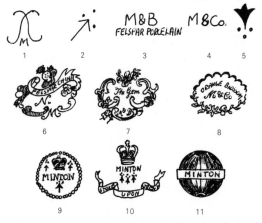

Naturally enough, early output consisted mostly of good quality transfer-printed earthenwares, and in the early 19th century the factory gained a high reputation largely due to the work of well-known painters, some of them from Derby. Among the wares for which the factory is renowned are white Parian figures, pâte-sur-pâte decoration on tinted grounds, fine almost egg-shell porcelain, and 'Majolica' wares.

Nantgarw China Works
Nantgarw, Glamorgan, c. 1813–14 and 1817–22.
1. Impressed mark 1813–22. The C.W. (for 'china works') is sometimes omitted, as is the space between the two parts of the word.
2. Painted written mark *c.* 1813–22. The word may also be stencilled, in upper-case letters, but cannot always be relied upon as authentic.

The factory, with Swansea, was at once the glory and the downfall of the perfectionist William Billingsley. His soft-paste body was incomparably lovely and wonderfully decorated, but ruinously expensive to produce. Because he left Wales to go to Coalport, there is a real danger of mistaking a superlative piece of Coalport porcelain for a piece of Swansea or Nantgarw, and the collector has to learn the details of true Welsh shapes and artists' characteristic styles, and to remember that the clinching Nantgarw mark, impressed and impossible to forge, is often practically obscured by glaze.

New Hall Porcelain Works
Shelton, Hanley, Staffordshire, 1781–1835.
1. Painted pattern numbers usually in red or more rarely in black, on 'hard paste' wares *c.* 1781–1812. Pattern numbers appear commonly without the N.
2. Printed mark on bone china *c.* 1812–35.

$\mathcal{N}$ 799

1

(New Hall)

2

Much New Hall porcelain was once called 'Cottage Bristol', and, in fact, the Bristol hard-paste factory was taken over by a company of Staffordshire potters in 1781. From the outset, apparently, after production began in the New Hall works, the decoration used was unlike anything done at Bristol, being slight and crude and applied to an inferior, greyer paste. The bone-ash paste used later is much whiter and more whitely translucent. Although most New Hall decoration is inferior, the factory was occasionally able to produce a really elaborate, well-painted pattern, with gilding of high quality, black-printing of the batt variety, and very occasionally printing in underglaze blue. The collector very quickly learns the distinctive moulded shapes of tea-wares in particular.

Pinxton Works
Pinxton, Derbyshire, c. 1796–1813.
1–3. Though Pinxton porcelain is rarely marked, these painted marks are sometimes seen. The P is sometimes found without a pattern number. After William Billingsley left the concern *c.* 1799, his partner John Coke used the crescent and star mark, together with various arrow symbols, until *c.* 1806.

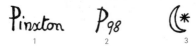

It may be supposed that here William Billingsley was first able to put his formulae to practical test, but in the more usual absence of marks the wares he made there are difficult to identify.

Plymouth Porcelain Works
Plymouth, Devon, under William Cookworthy, 1768–70.
1 & 2.   Painted 'tin symbol' marks in underglaze blue or enamels *c.* 1768–70. Also to be found on Samson imitations.
3.   Impressed mark of the 'repairer' Tebo, found also on Bristol, Bow and Worcester wares.

$$2\!\!\!+ \qquad 2\!\!\!/ \qquad T^{\circ}$$

1   2   3

See the notes under Bristol, because William Cookworthy moved from Plymouth to Bristol in 1770, and in 1773 left the business to his partner Richard Champion.

Rockingham Works
Nr. Swinton, Yorkshire, c. 1745–1842.
Porcelain was not made here until *c.* 1826, and thereafter the standard 'griffin' mark was used, at first in red until 1830, and then in puce, with various alterations to the wording beneath. Thus: 'Royal Rockingham Works' instead of 'Rockingham Works' and/or
(contd.)

31

'China Manufacturers to the King' *c.* 1830–42, and 'Manufacturers to the Queen' *c.* 1837 onwards. Very rarely an impressed ROCKINGHAM WORKS, BRAMELD or ROCKINGHAM BRAMELD is seen on porcelain *c.* 1826–30.

A great deal of Rockingham porcelain is so lavishly and expensively decorated that the factory could not have survived without the patronage of Earl Fitzwilliam. Unmarked Staffordshire porcelain is often called 'Rockingham', which is one reason why pieces bearing the 'Griffin' mark are held in high regard.

Spode

Stoke-on-Trent, Staffordshire. Josiah Spode c. 1784–1833, Copeland & Garrett 1833–47, W. T. Copeland & Sons Ltd. 1847 to the present day.

1. Early workman's mark, painted in gold *c.* 1790–1805.
2. A rare impressed mark on early wares *c.* 1784–1805, and in printed form *c.* 1805 onwards.
3. Written mark, usually in red, followed by a pattern number *c.* 1790–1820.
4. Printed in several styles, in puce or black on felspar porcelains *c.* 1815–27.
5. Impressed *c.* 1784–1805.
6. Printed *c.* 1847–51, and with the Cs elaborated 1851–1885.
7. Printed 1875–90.
8. One of the many self-explanatory printed marks of the period *c.* 1833–47.

(contd.)

| 5 | 6 | 7 | 8 |

Throughout its life the Spode factory, under any management, has never made anything of poor quality, and hardly any style of decoration has not been attempted. The collector is well-advised to visit the collections on view at the Stoke factory.

Swansea

Swansea, Wales, 1814–22.

1. Impressed, written or printed 1814–22. In the impressed form, may be accompanied by a trident or two crossed tridents to indicate use of the 'trident paste'.
2. Impressed, sometimes with the word SWAN-SEA, *c.* 1814–17.
3. Painted 1814–22.

N.B. No. 1 is suspect in printed form, because the copper plates used to produce it became the property of the Coalport concern in 1822, and it is possible that they may well have been used there to mark the particularly fine porcelain made to Billingsley's recipes.

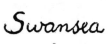

1   2

3

Much Swansea may be approximately dated by the kind of paste used, since Billingsley was obliged to make repeated efforts to save expense owing to kiln losses. Thus, in about 1816 the 'duck-egg' paste, greenly translucent, was introduced, to be followed shortly afterwards by the still cheaper 'trident body', which did not please the London china dealers.

Josiah Wedgwood & Sons Ltd.
Burslem c. 1759, Etruria c. 1769, Barlaston 1940.
1. Printed, very small, in red, blue or gold on bone china *c.* 1812–22.
2. Printed mark of the 'Portland Vase' from *c.* 1878. 'ENGLAND' added below from 1891. A similar mark, but with the body of the vase left white, and with three stars beneath it, was used from *c.* 1900. The words BONE CHINA were added *c.* 1920 and in 1962 the body of the vase was again filled in.

WEDGWOOD

WEDGWOOD

1   2

Josiah Wedgwood was a perfectionist, and from the beginning the name of Wedgwood has always been synonymous with quality, so that while many Staffordshire potters imitated, for example, his jasper and cream-ware, their products were for the most part of poorer quality.

Worcester
For convenience sake the marks of all the various factories and companies in Worcester are placed together. Their dates are as follows:

THE MAIN FACTORY, *c. 1751.*
First (or Dr. Wall) Period, 1751–1783.
Davis/Flight or Middle Period, 1776–1793.
Barr and Flight & Barr Period, 1792–1807.
Barr Flight & Barr Period, 1807–13.
Flight Barr & Barr Period, 1813–40.
CHAMBERLAINS & CO., *c. 1786–1852.*
KERR & BINNS, *1852–62.*
GRAINGERS, *c. 1812–1902.*
HADLEYS, *1896–1905.*
LOCKES, *1895–1904.*
WORCESTER ROYAL PORCELAIN CO., *1862* to present day.

Worcester

FIRST PERIOD

1–4. Crescent marks c. 1755–90, in underglaze blue.

1. Open painted crescent found on wares painted in underglaze blue, or may rarely be found on enamelled wares, in gold or enamel.

2–4. Printed, on wares in underglaze blue. Several other capital letters are found inside the crescent, which may also be found, rarely, in the shape of a face. Continued into the Davis/Flight period.

5. The fretted square, painted in underglaze blue *c.* 1755–1770 on wares painted in underglaze blue, in several similar forms. Rarely accompanied by the crescent.

6–9. Painted or printed, according to whether the piece is painted or printed in underglaze blue, *c.* 1755–70.

10 & 11. Pseudo-Chinese marks painted in underglaze blue, many variations, *c.* 1753–70.

12–14. The Meissen 'crossed swords', painted in underglaze blue, usually found on wares painted in the Meissen style, *c.* 1760–70, but also found on pieces printed overglaze in puce enamel.

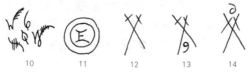

Worcester

First period (contd.).

15–17.   On pieces printed in overglaze enamel. The RH refers to the engraver and printer Robert Hancock, and the anchor is the rebus of Richard Holdship, a former proprietor of the factory.

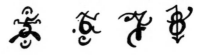

15   16   17

18.   Examples of numbers disguised as Chinese characters, and so known as 'disguised numerals', found on wares made *c.* 1775–90, printed in underglaze blue on certain types of blue-printed wares formerly attributed to the Caughley factory.

18

19.   Examples of workmen's or painters' marks painted on early underglaze blue-painted wares *c.* 1751–65.

19

Worcester

DAVIS/FLIGHT PERIOD, 1783–93

20. Painted in blue, 1783–8. A crescent alone, smaller than that used during the First Period, is also found.

21. A crown was added after the King's visit in 1788.

22. Found in various forms, painted in blue.

| 20 | 21 | 22 |

BARR AND FLIGHT & BARR PERIOD, *c.* 1793–1807

23. Incised, usually on tea wares.

24. Written mark found in various forms. Also, several self-explanatory painted or printed marks.

| 23 | 24 |

BARR FLIGHT & BARR PERIOD, *c.* 1807–13

25. Impressed, often accompanied by self-explanatory written or printed marks, sometimes with London addresses and Royal warrant.

25

FLIGHT BARR & BARR PERIOD, *c.* 1813–40

26. Impressed, and also as above.

26

Worcester
CHAMBERLAINS

27. Early mark, *c.* 1786–1810, found in many forms.

27   *Chamberlains*

Between *c.* 1811 and 1840 many self-explanatory printed and written marks were used, some with London addresses, Royal warrants and crowns. Note that the words 'Regent China' denote a special body or paste used for expensive wares. *c.* 1811–20.

28. Impressed or printed, with or without 'Worcester', *c.* 1847–50.

29. Printed, *c.* 1850–52.

CHAMBERLAINS

28

29

KERR & BINNS PERIOD, 1852–62

30. Printed or impressed. The crown added in 1862.

31. Shield mark *c.* 1854–62. The last two numerals of the year in the central bar, the artist's initials or signature in the bottom L.H. corner.

30

31

GRAINGERS, *c.* 1812–1902
Grainger, Lee & Co. c. 1812–c. 1839, then George Grainger & Co. c. 1839–1902.

32. In several painted or printed forms.

33. Painted or printed in several forms, *c.* 1812–39.

34. Printed or impressed, *c.* 1870–89.

George Grainger
Royal China Works
Worcester

32

Grainger **Lee** & Co.
Worcester

33

34

The same form of mark, with 'Royal China Works' above and 'Worcester' below, was used *c.* 1889–1902, and the word 'England' was added from 1891, when date letters were also added below, commencing with A.

Worcester

HADLEYS, 1896–1905

35. Incised or impressed on pieces modelled by James Hadley for the Worcester Royal Porcelain Company, *c.* 1875–94.

36. Printed or impressed, 1896–97.

37. Printed, Aug. 1902–June 30th, 1905.

 35 36 37

Various other self-explanatory marks also used.

LOCKES, 1895–1904

Founded by Edward Locke in the Shrub Hill Works, to make porcelain in the Royal Worcester style, and closed after a law action with the Royal Worcester company.

38. Printed mark, *c.* 1895–1900.

 38

WORCESTER ROYAL PORCELAIN COMPANY, 1862 – present day

The Flight Barr and Barr concern amalgamated with Chamberlains in 1840, and in 1852 reorganisation resulted in the foundation of a new company known as Kerr and Binns. When Kerr retired in 1862 the modern W.R.P.C. was formed. Note that Graingers were taken over in 1889 and Hadleys in 1905.

THE STANDARD MARK

1862–75. The standard Kerr and Binns mark (30) was taken over, with an open crown above and a C in the centre instead of a crescent. Two numerals below denote the last two numerals of the year, and from 1867 a system of date letters was used, as follows:

A 1867	G 1872	M 1877	T 1882	Y 1887
B 1868	H 1873	N 1878	U 1883	Z 1888
C 1869	I 1874	P 1879	V 1884	O 1889
D 1870	K 1875	R 1880	W 1885	a 1890
E 1871	L 1876	S 1881	X 1886	

Worcester

Worcester Royal Porcelain Company (contd.).

1876–91. The same mark, but with a crescent replacing the C in the centre, and the crown filled in. Year letters commencing with 'a' for 1890, as above. This mark is also found in impressed form, without year letters.

1891 onwards. The same mark, with 'Royal Worcester, England' added. 'Made in England' denotes a 20th century origin.

A complicated system of arrangements of dots to denote year of manufacture was adopted from 1892, which may be referred to in G. A. Godden's 'Encyclopaedia' of marks.

The standard mark has been revised from time to time, but is always self-explanatory.

Much of the early ware is unmarked, and even later, at Chamberlains and at Flights, the only mark on a service may be inside a tea-pot lid, sucrier cover, or beneath a single dish of a dinner or dessert service. The earliest 'blue and white' may bear either a workman's mark or a crescent, W or fretted square. With few exceptions it is unusual to find a mark on First Period enamelled pieces which have no underglaze blue in their decoration probably because the painter who applied the underglaze blue could conveniently also apply the mark in the same colour.

Earthenware Marks

William Adams & Sons (Potters) Ltd.
This concern, also known under several earlier titles, is perhaps best known of the many Adams firms working in the Potteries during the 18th and 19th centuries. Founded c. 1769
1.   Impressed, 1787–1805 on Jasper wares, 1800–64 on earthenwares, with '& Co.' 1769–1800. Also on Parian figures 1845–64.
2.   Printed, from 1896 onwards.
3.   Printed, with pattern name. 1819–64. The initials below are found as a part of many other printed marks.
4.   Printed mark on wares made for the American market *c.* 1830–50.

1 **ADAMS**

 2

3

 4

The finest Adams product is perhaps the blue jasper ware, violet toned, and often less frigidly modelled than the Wedgwood variety which it imitated. It should be remembered that William Adams was a friend and favourite pupil of Wedgwood and a modeller of exceptional merit.

Edward Asbury & Co.
Longton. 1875–1925.
Printed mark 1875–1925. Also found with the names ASBURY and LONGTON.

H. Aynsley & Co. Ltd.
Longton. 1873 onwards.
An example of the Staffordshire Knot mark used by many potters, usually with distinguishing initials similarly arranged, and with ENGLAND added from 1891 onwards.

Another Aynsley, named John, had a pottery in Longton from about 1864, making mostly porcelain but also lustre wares, bearing self-explanatory marks incorporating only the surname.

J. & M. P. Bell & Co. Ltd.
Glasgow Pottery. 1842–1928.
1 & 2. Impressed or printed, with the addition of LTD or LD from 1881.

1   2

Belle Vue Pottery
Hull. Various proprietors from c. 1802.
The 'Two Bells' mark, printed or impressed *c.* 1826–41.

The original partnership was between Jeremiah and James Smith and Job Ridgway, until 1804 when Ridgway retired. The chief productions were domestic earthenware, green-glazed and blue-printed ware.

Bishop & Stonier Ltd.
Hanley. 1891–1939. Formerly Powell, Bishop & Stonier.
Printed mark 1880–1936, after which date it was impressed. The initials B & S were also used in printed or impressed form, and there are several later (after *c.* 1899) self-explanatory printed marks.

Booths Limited
Tunstall. 1891–1948.
Printed mark found on earthenware reproductions of First Period Worcester 'blue and white' porcelains. The fretted square of the same factory is also sometimes found. Enamelled reproductions are not commonly marked.

Booth reproductions are remarkably accurate as regards decoration, but are betrayed by their natural opacity, and, in the case of larger pieces such as openwork baskets in the enamelled Worcester style, by creaminess of paste and lightness of weight.

Bristol. Pountney & Co. Ltd.
c. 1849 onwards.
1 & 2. 1849–1889, and other marks incorporating initials or names.
3. 1884 on pieces specially glazed. The numerals below indicate month and year of manufacture. Ltd. added after 1889.

P. & CO. 1   **POUNTNEY & CO.** 2   **BRISTOL** +2/84 3

(contd.)

Cream-ware was first made in Bristol, in about 1786, by Joseph Ring, who engaged potters from Shelton in the Potteries. Notable flower-painters were William Fifield (1777–1857) and his son John, who continued to work with the Pountneys. Many pieces, brightly painted by them for Pountney and Allies, including distinctive small barrels, bear the name and date of the person for whom they were made.

Bristol. Pountney & Allies

c. 1816–35.

1 & 2.   Printed, impressed or painted, *c.* 1816–35.

3.   Impressed, *c.* 1816–35.

4.   Printed in blue *c.* 1825.

5.   Impressed 1816–35.

6.   Printed in blue *c.* 1830.

P. & A   BRISTOL POTTERY

1   2   3

   POUNTNEY & ALLIES

4   5   6

Britannia Pottery Co. Ltd.

Glasgow, formerly Cochran & Fleming. 1896–1935.
Several forms of the printed seated Britannia mark, side-face or full-face, 1896–1920. Later forms have self-explanatory lettering.

There were in fact many late 19th century potteries in Glasgow, all making the usual ironstones, cream-ware, stoneware and general domestic ware of the period.

Brown Westhead, Moore & Co.

Hanley. 1862–1904.

Printed mark 1862 onwards. The initials, or the name in full, are found in various printed or impressed marks, sometimes with a pattern name. The word CAULDON appears in marks used *c.* 1890.

They were the successors, after many partnerships, to the Ridgways – Job, John and William – who began business in 1802. W. Moore had been assistant to John Ridgway. The earthenwares, Majolica, and Parian wares won the highest awards at many Exhibitions throughout the world, being, in the words of J. F. Blacker, 'peculiarly good, hard, compact and durable, and the patterns chaste and effective'. Note that old Cauldon ware was marked with such marks as I. RIDGWAY, RIDGWAY & SONS and JOHN RIDGWAY & CO.

Davenport

Longport. c. 1793–1887.

1 & 2. Impressed, the name sometimes accompanied by an anchor. Lower case letters 1793–1810, upper case letters after 1805.

3. Printed on stone china, *c.* 1805–20.

4. Printed, *c.* 1795, sometimes with LONGPORT instead of DAVENPORT. A later version was used up to about 1860, sometimes with the last two numerals of the year on either side of the anchor.

5. Impressed, on wares of all periods. Many other Davenport marks are self-explanatory.

1	2	3	4	5

John Davenport was an artistic potter, and is better known for his porcelain, which bears similar marks to those reproduced here. His blue-printed earthenwares are particularly fine, with perforated rims to plates and dishes, and he made stone china in the Mason style, as, for example, his octagonal jugs. Decoration is usually strong in colour, with occasional fine gilding, and some excellent painting of fruit was done, probably by Steele of Derby.

William de Morgan

Chelsea, Fulham etc. London. c. 1872–1907.

1. An example of the several name marks used *c.* 1882 onwards. '& Co.' added after 1888.
2. Impressed or painted, 1882 onwards.

1   2

William de Morgan may be classed with Bernard Moore and W. Howson Taylor of 'Ruskin' fame as a studio potter who was inspired by the brilliant strength of colour of ancient Continental or Oriental wares, in de Morgan's case by the fine lustre effects on old Majolica and the intense blues of old Persian wares.

J. Dimmock & Co.

Hanley. 1862–1904.

1. Printed monogram mark, 1862–78; sometimes the same initials are found with pattern names.
2–4. Printed, *c.* 1878–1904. From *c.* 1878 the name of the new proprietor D. D. Cliff was used in many printed marks.

This firm originated in about 1816, when the son of Wedgwood's modeller, Hackwood, entered into partnership with John Dimmock to make earthenware.

47

Don Pottery
Swinton, Yorkshire. 1790–1893.
1. Impressed or painted *c.* 1790–1830.
2. Impressed or painted, 1820–34. Another version bears the words GREEN DON POTTERY.

DON POTTERY

1

2

An almost unknown pottery until about 1800, when one of the brothers Green, of Leeds, became owner, so that many finest pieces made at Swinton were in fact of Leeds design.

Doulton & Co. Ltd.
Lambeth and Burslem. c. 1858–1956. The Lambeth works closed in 1956, while the Burslem works continued.
1. Impressed, *c.* 1858 onwards. The same words are sometimes found impressed in an oval or, rarely, in a circle, with the year of manufacture between them.
2 & 7. Painted or impressed *c.* 1882–1902, with ENGLAND after 1891.
3. Impressed or printed, *c.* 1887–1900.
4. Impressed *c.* 1881–1912, with ENGLAND after 1891.
5. Impressed or printed *c.* 1872 onwards.
6. Impressed, *c.* 1888–98.
8. The standard impressed Doulton mark, found in several forms from *c.* 1902 onwards. MADE IN ENGLAND added in 1891.

1 2 3 4

DOULTON LAMBETH

(contd.)

5   6   7   8

This revival of artistic stoneware was begun by Henry Doulton, the intention being to make domestic vessels as ornamental as the old Flemish ware. Actually a stoneware works was founded by John Doulton at Vauxhall in 1815, afterwards being carried on by Doulton and Watts before being transferred to High Street, Lambeth, some years later. At the 1851 Exhibition the Lambeth terra-cotta wares were highly commended, but it was some 20 years later that the use of sgraffito (scratched) designs typical of Doulton ware were developed, while different coloured bodies were gradually introduced. Nineteenth century Doulton ware may be divided roughly into the following classes: salt-glazed stoneware, usually simply called 'Doulton Ware'; chiné ware (faience either salt or lead-glazed), silicon ware, which is vitrified stoneware without a salt glaze, but making use of coloured clays; Carrara Ware which is covered with a transparent crystalline enamel; marqueterie ware made of marbled clays in chequered designs; Lambeth faience which is a terra-cotta or biscuit body bearing underglaze painting, and glazed faience mostly used for larger vases, architectural decoration and tiles. A considerable number of skilled artists was employed to decorate these wares, notably including the Barlow sisters and George Tinworth, whose work is usually signed with their monograms.

Thomas Fell & Co. Ltd.
St. Peter's Pottery, Newcastle-upon-Tyne. 1817–90.
Impressed marks, 1817–30. Between 1830 and 1890, initials or Christian name initial and full surname were impressed or printed in several forms, '& Co.' being added later.

1   2   3   4

A large group of potteries were situated on the rivers Tyne, Wear and Tees, mostly at Newcastle and Sunderland, and their wares had a predominately nautical flavour, carried out in washed-in black transfer, often with pink lustre ornamentation. This can be seen in the well-known 'Wear Bridge' jugs, bowls and mugs made by Dixon and Co. of Sunderland. Most of these potters, including Fell, marked some of their products with name marks.

Gildea & Walker
Burslem. 1881–5.
The mark first used by predecessors Bates Elliott & Co.
c. 1870 but without the words TRADE MARK, and
afterwards, *c.* 1885–8, within a double circle, by
successors James Gildea. The figure of the potter is to
be found in various forms of the mark.

T. G. Green & Co. Ltd.
Church Gresley, Nr. Burton-on-Trent. c. 1864 onwards.
The printed 'church mark', first registered in 1888
and used in various forms afterwards. ENGLAND
added after 1891.

Hicks, Meigh & Johnson
Shelton. 1822–35.
Printed mark *c.* 1822–35, but possibly used also by
Hicks & Meigh (1806–22). The three initial letters
appear in various other printed marks.

Specialising in transfer-printing under and over the glaze, and particularly in
deep dark blue underglaze.

Hilditch & Son
Lane End. 1822–30.
Various forms of printed marks bearing initials.

Samuel Hollins
Shelton. c. 1784–1813.
Impressed marks, but many pieces are unmarked.

*S.*HOLLINS

HOLLINS

Noteworthy for his red and chocolate-coloured unglazed stoneware decorated with raised designs in the Elers style, and for green stoneware tea and coffee-pots decorated with applied blue jasper ornament. Many of these designs were copied from silver shapes. The use of lustre bands, particularly around the rims of mugs and tankards, and not unlike gun-metal in appearance, was a speciality of Hollins, one of the early proprietors of the New Hall porcelain works.

Johnson Bros. (Hanley) Ltd.
Hanley, from 1883, and at Tunstall c. 1899–1913.
Most marks, impressed or printed, are of this name mark type, and some incorporate pattern names.

Lowesby Pottery
Leicestershire. c. 1835–40.
1 & 2.   Impressed, *c.* 1835–40.
3.   Printed, *c.* 1835–40.

LOWESBY

1

2

3

Under Sir Francis Fowke, red terra-cotta ware covered with dull black was manufactured, and brightly painted with enamels, this painting possibly not being done in the actual factory.

Leeds Pottery
Hunslet, Leeds, under various proprietors. c. 1758–1880.
1.   Impressed, *c.* 1775–*c.* 1800. The same words in lower case letters on printed creamware *c.* 1790 onwards.
2 & 3.   Impressed, *c.* 1781–1820.

LEEDS POTTERY

1

HARTLEY, GREENS & CO.

2

HARTLEY GREENS & CO
LEEDS•POTTERY

3

Although ordinary earthenwares and black basalts were made by the various proprietors, the fame of Leeds rests upon its fine cream-ware, much of which is unmarked. At first imitative of Wedgwood ware and intending to rival porcelain in lightness, durability and cheapness, the best Leeds cream-ware often surpasses Wedgwood in its design and technical excellence. Much is finely pierced and so greatly admired by collectors, that it is often forged. But modern copies lack the fine potting, are heavier in weight, and have a thick, white, glassy glaze unlike that of true Leeds, which has a greenish tint in the crevices.

Martin Brothers
Fulham and Southall, London. 1873–1914. The brothers were Robert Wallace, Walter, Edwin and Charles.
1. Incised, 1873–4. C3 refers to the model.
2. Incised, 1874–78. Note that the letter before the numeral is discontinued.
3. Incised, *c.* 1878–9.
4. Incised, *c.* 1879–82.

All four brothers had formal artistic training, and Walter and Edwin had been employed at Doultons. Although their productions of salt-glazed stoneware included everyday vases, bottles, bowls, jugs, etc. in the Doulton style, their fame rests most upon their grotesque, sometimes almost ugly caricatures of human faces, birds and beasts in the shape of jugs and other suitable forms.

Charles James Mason & Co.
Patent Ironstone China Manufactory, Lane Delph. 1829–45. Previously G. M. and C. J. Mason, and subsequently C. J. Mason.
1 & 2.   Versions of the standard Ironstone mark used by G. M. and C. J. Mason 1813–29, and subsequently throughout the life of the factory, being used after 1862 by Ashworths who later added their own name. The word IMPROVED occurs *c.* 1840.

(contd.)

3. A version of the basic mark, but without the scroll, *c.* 1845.

4. Printed mark *c.* 1825, with pattern numbers beneath. There are several other printed marks of the period 1829–45 using the same words.

'Mason's Patent Ironstone China' was introduced in an attempt to provide the industrial middle-class with a cheap, durable, colourful substitute for the splendid Chinese porcelain owned by the wealthy. Articles made included enormous vases, some of them replicas of the Oriental, fireplace surrounds, bed-posts, large dinner-services and, of course, many sizes of the typical octagonal jug with snake or dragon handle. Much of the decoration was transferred and washed in with enamels, and the sometimes garish blues, reds and greens enriched with gilding of good quality. Occasionally one finds better pieces bearing panels of well-painted landscape or flowers. A class of ware which is seldom marked is completely covered with a deep blue enamel (which usually trespasses a little upon the white base of the article), upon which decoration is applied in gold, sometimes tooled, in bright enamels, or in a combination of both.

Elijah Mayer
Cobden Works, Hanley. c. *1790–1804. Succeeded by Elijah Mayer & Son, 1805–34.*
1. Impressed, *c.* 1790–1804.
2. Impressed or printed, 1805–34.

E. MAYER   **'E. Mayer & Son'**

Middlesborough Pottery Co.
Middlesborough-on-Tees. 1834–44.
An example of the anchor mark, found either with initials or with the name in full, which in turn may be found without the anchor.

Minton

Stoke, under various names. 1793 onwards.

1. Moulded, on moulded wares *c.* 1830–40.
2. Printed, *c.* 1900–8.

Many printed marks and year cyphers are found on both earthenware and porcelain bodies, c.f. porcelain marks section and Appendix.

1   2

Thomas Minton (1765–1836) was formerly an engraver at Spodes, after serving an apprenticeship at Caughley under Thomas Turner, for whom he engraved several underglaze-blue designs, including the well-known 'Broseley Dragon'. 'Stone China' was made at Mintons, very similar to that introduced by Mason, decorated mainly in Oriental style, as in the case of the famous 'Amherst Japan' pattern made in honour of Lord Amherst, Governor General of India.

Bernard Moore

Wolfe Street, Stoke. 1905–15.

1. Painted mark found in various forms, 1905–15.
2. Painted or printed, sometimes with the year, 1905–15.

Bernard Moore's factory should not be confused with that of the Moore Brothers (1872–1905) who preceded him, and whose wares bear self-explanatory impressed or printed marks.

B MOORE

1   2

Few potters have imitated so successfully the Chinese 'sang-de-boeuf', plain or flambé, sometimes bearing designs in blue, black, turquoise, gold and other bright colours. Moore was able to produce a wide range of splashed or transmutation glazes, including a fine 'peach-bloom', often as brilliant as the true Chinese.

Myatt Pottery Co.

Bilston, Staffs.

The impressed mark, registered in 1880 and used until *c.* 1894.

Not to be confused with the name mark used by other potters of the same name working in the Potteries during the late 18th and 19th centuries.

James Neale & Co.

Church Works, Hanley. c. 1776–c. 1786. Subsequently Messrs. Neale & Wilson and, in 1795, Robert Wilson.

1. Impressed mark of James Neale & Co., *c.* 1776–86. Impressed initials and names also used.
2. Impressed, with crescent or G, used by Neale & Co., *c.* 1780–90.
3. Impressed, *c.* 1784–95.
4. Impressed, *c.* 1795–1800.

NEALE & WILSON

3

WILSON

1   2   4

Makers of fine figures, usually in the classical style, since the famous French modeller Voyez worked at the factory. In addition, stoneware jugs with cupids in relief, baskets and, rather later, after Wilson joined the firm, an improved cream-ware, silver lustre and pink lustre in the Wedgwood style.

Pearson & Co.

Chesterfield. Est. 1805.

Impressed or printed, *c.* 1880. Before this date impressed marks P & CO or the name in full.

Benjamin Plant
Lane End, Longton. c. 1780–1820.
Incised mark *c.* 1780–1820. Many other potters of the
same name worked in Staffordshire towards the end
of the 19th century, for the most part using name
marks.

BPlant
Lane End.

Portobello
Near Edinburgh. c. 1764 onwards.
Mark of Thomas Rathbone & Co., from 1810
onwards. Other Portobello potters were Scott
Brothers 1786–96 and A. W. Buchan & Co. Ltd.,
from 1867 onwards, whose marks are self-explanatory.

TR&Cº

F. & R. Pratt & Co. Ltd.
*Fenton. Est. c. 1818. Taken over by the Cauldon Potteries
Ltd. in the 1920's. Formerly Felix Pratt.*
1. Printed, *c.* 1818–60. Other marks are initials, and
initials with '& Co' added *c.* 1840.
2 & 3. Printed, on coloured transfer-printed wares
of the 'Pot Lid' type, sometimes with pattern
numbers.

PRATT	PRATT FENTON	F&R PRATTS 268 FENTON
1	2	3

Above all, a company noted for the production of underglaze printed lids of
pomade-pots called 'Pot Lids', and of dessert services and other domestic
wares upon which the same pot-lid prints were often used. Many engravers,
such as the William Brooke mentioned by Simeon Shaw and Austin of Pratts,
did much to develop the new process, in which every colour was printed
separately, each being allowed to dry for a day or so, in contrast to the quicker
and cheaper lithographic process.

Rockingham Works
Swinton, Yorkshire. c. *1745–1842.*
1. An impressed mark of John and William Brameld, c. 1778–1842. Many other impressed marks, some including the word ROCKINGHAM.
2. Impressed, c. 1806 onwards.
3. Relief mark, c. 1806 onwards.

BRAMELD

1

ROCKINGHAM

2

3

Best known of the earthenware made at Swinton is the brown-glazed cream-
ware used extensively between about 1796 and 1806, and usually called
'Rockingham Ware', though in fact it was made also at other Staffordshire
potteries. Among typical pieces are many kinds of brandy flasks in the shapes,
for example, of shoes, pistols, etc., Toby jugs, and the famous peach-shaped
'Cadogan' tea-pot.

Royal Essex Pottery
Also known as Hedingham Art Pottery. Castle Hedingham, Essex. 1864–1901.
Applied mark in relief used 1864–1901 on so-called 'Castle Hedingham' wares, and often removed in fraudulent attempts to pass them off as much earlier pieces. An incised mark including the proprietor's name also found.

Ralph Salt
Marsh Street, Hanley. c. 1820–46.
Impressed on scroll in relief on the backs of bases of figures.

SALT

Salt was born in 1782 and died in 1846, and was one of the most notable figure-makers in the Walton style, his models being similar in design and in colouring, though he occasionally used metallic lustre either by itself or with enamels. A feature of some of his figures is the title impressed on the front of the base.

Scott Brothers
Portobello, Nr. Edinburgh. c. 1786–96.
An example of the various impressed name marks.

SCOTT BROS

Shorthose & Heath
Hanley. c. 1795–1815.
Impressed or printed *c.* 1795–1815.

SHORTHOSE &
HEATH

Shorthose & Co.
Hanley. Successors to Shorthose & Heath. c. 1817–1822.
Printed in blue on blue-printed wares. The name mark without the crescents is also found, in upper case letters, in impressed, printed and painted forms.

Shorthose &Co
CC

Notably makers of white earthenware printed overglaze in red, rustic subjects such as 'Children at Play', and of cream-ware including plates and dishes with embossed wicker-work pierced rims.

Spodes

Stoke-on-Trent. Various titles – Josiah Spode c. 1784–1833, Copeland & Garrett 1833–47, W. T. Copeland & Sons, Ltd., 1847 to present day.

1 & 2. Impressed on blue-printed wares, *c.* 1784–1800.
3. Impressed on the 'New Stone' body, *c.* 1805–20.
4. Printed in black *c.* 1805–15, in blue *c.* 1815–30.
5–7. Printed, *c.* 1805–33.
8. Printed, 1867–90.

Among the many achievements of this great pottery were the great advances made in the process of transfer printing, not only in underglaze-blue, but also in colour, particularly when applied to the durable stone chinas. Much use was made of printed outline which was then filled in with enamels in many different colour schemes to give wide ranges of cheaply produced patterns.

Andrew Stevenson

Cobridge. c. 1816–30.

1. Impressed, *c.* 1816–30, and also found with initial.
2. Impressed, *c.* 1820.
3. Impressed, *c.* 1816–30.

Ralph Stevenson
Cobridge. c. 1810–32.
One of numerous impressed marks. Sometimes the initials only, and sometimes with '& Son'.

R. STEVENSON

Stevenson & Williams
Cobridge. c. 1825. According to Godden, a partnership between Ralph Stevenson and Aldborough Lloyd Williams.
1. Printed mark.
2. Printed mark on pieces decorated with American views.

Stubbs & Kent
Longport. c. 1828–30.
Impressed or printed. Also used by Joseph Stubbs of Longport, who was probably connected in some way with this firm. His wares usually bear impressed name marks, and may be dated *c.* 1822–35.

Swansea

Cambrian Pottery. c. *1783–1870.*
1–4. Impressed, *c.* 1783–*c.* 1810.
5. Impressed or printed, *c.* 1811–17, in various forms.
6. Impressed, *c.* 1824–50.
7. Printed, *c.* 1862–70, in various forms.

SWANSEA   **CAMBRIA**

1   2

CAMBRIAN   **CAMBRIAN POTTERY**

3   4

DILLWYN & CO.   **DILLWYN**

5   6

D. J. EVANS & CO.

7

It should be noted that for part of this time a rival pottery at Glamorgan (*c.* 1814–39) made 'opaque china' and cream-ware. Among Cambrian Pottery products were fine black basalt, underglaze blue-painted, blue-printed and black-printed wares, a red earthenware impressed with classical subjects in black called 'Dillwyn's Etruscan Ware' made between 1847 and 1850, and above all, an improved, whiter cream-ware enamelled by W. W. Young, Thomas Pardoe, and other outstanding artists.

W. Howson Taylor

Ruskin Pottery, Smethwick, Birmingham. 1898–1935.
1. Impressed, *c.* 1898–early 19th century.
2 & 3. Painted or incised of the same period. Later marks are self-explanatory.

TAYLOR

1   2   3

Howson Taylor's 'Ruskin' pottery was an attempt to rival Chinese coloured glazes in every colour from white to sang-de-boeuf, often with fine flambé effects.

Charles Tittensor
Shelton. c. 1815–23. Various partnerships.
Printed on printed wares, and impressed on very rare figures.

TITTENSOR

Maker of figures with bocage or tree backgrounds which may be looked upon as transitional between the Wood coloured glaze ones and the enamelled variety of Walton and Salt. The few authentic specimens known are rather crudely modelled and enamelled in attractive blue, green, yellow and orange-yellow.

John Turner
Lane End, Longton. c. 1762–1806. Not to be confused with Thomas Turner of Caughley.
1.   Impressed mark from *c.* 1770 onwards, usually on stonewares.
2.   Printed or impressed from 1784, sometimes with the name beneath.

TURNER

1

2

One of Wedgwood's rivals in the making of fine jasper wares in the classical style, and a maker of fine stoneware of warm biscuit tint, sharply modelled in relief, and often enhanced with bands of blue or brown enamel. His black basalts are equal to those of Wedgwood and he is said to have been a pioneer of underglaze-blue printing in the Potteries.

John Voyez
Staffordshire modeller to Ralph and other members of the Wood family. c. 1768–1800.
An example of the various impressed name marks, on such modelled specimens as the 'Fair Hebe' jugs.

J. VOYEZ

A typical example of the nomadic craftsman who worked for many potters, including Wedgwood and Neale & Co.

John Walton

Burslem. c. 1818–35.

Impressed mark on a relief scroll on the backs of bocage figures.

Probably the most important potter to follow the figure-making tradition of the Woods, making gay, colourful and attractive figures with bocage backgrounds in emulation of Chelsea and Derby porcelain. His pieces were intended to be the poor man's porcelain, and were designed to stand against the wall and so to be viewed only from the front. His range of subjects was wide – religious, historical, sporting, and rustic, and he was wont to assemble a series of stock motifs, such as cows, dogs, sheep or human figures into different composite models.

John Warburton

Cobridge. c. 1802–25.

Impressed. The name is also found, but usually with the addition of initials and/or place names, on wares made by others of the same name, e.g. John Warburton of Gateshead *c.* 1750–95, Peter Warburton of Cobridge *c.* 1802–12, and Peter and Francis Warburton of Cobridge *c.* 1795–1802.

WARBURTON

Watson's Pottery

Prestonpans, Scotland. c. 1750–1840.

Impressed, *c.* 1770–1800. Self explanatory marks thereafter.

WATSON

Josiah Wedgwood & Sons, Ltd.

Burslem c. 1759, Etruria c. 1769, Barlaston 1940.

1–3. Impressed marks. 1 and 3 *c.* 1759–69, and 2 the standard mark *c.* 1759 onwards. From 1860 a three-

(contd.)

letter dating system was used, and from 1891 'ENGLAND' was added. 'MADE IN ENGLAND' signifies a 20th century origin.

Wedgwood   **WEDGWOOD**   WEDGWOOD

1   2   3

4. Impressed on ornamental wares of the Wedgwood and Bentley period, *c.* 1768–80.

WEDGWOOD & BENTLEY

4

5. Impressed on small cameos, plaques etc., Wedgwood and Bentley period, *c.* 1768–80.

W & B

5

6. Impressed or in relief on vases etc. of the Wedgwood and Bentley period, *c.* 1768–80.

6

7. Modern mark, impressed, *c.* 1929 onwards.

WEDGWOOD

7

8 & 9. Misleading marks of Wedgwood & Co. Ltd., Unicorn and Pinnox Works, Tunstall, *c.* 1860 onwards, and John Wedge Wood of Burslem and Tunstall, *c.* 1845–60.

WEDGWOOD & CO.

8

J. WEDGWOOD

9

Apart from his fame as a developer of the classical spirit in his wonderful jasper ware, Wedgwood also brought cream-ware to a high standard of excellence for domestic use. He also invented or improved variegated wares imitating marble and other natural stones, the red ware called 'rosso antico' which was sometimes decorated with bright enamels, and the well-known, clean-looking 'cauliflower' wares.

Enoch Wood
Burslem. c. 1784–1790.
1–3. Examples of the various name marks on domestic wares, figures, plaques etc. Though a modeller of note, he did not set up a factory of his own until 1784.

ENOCH WOOD
SCULPSET

E WOOD

Enoch Wood &Co

1   2   3

Known in his day as the 'Father of the Potteries', and a capable potter and modeller beside being one of the first recorded students and actual collectors of early pottery. He is best known for his portrait busts in black basalt, black-enamelled creamware and painted creamware, and his vast output also included blue-printed earthenwares bearing landscapes and figure subjects intended for the American market.

Wood & Caldwell
Burslem. c. 1790–1818. Successors to Enoch Wood.
Impressed mark.

WOOD & CALDWELL

Enoch Wood & Sons
Burslem. 1818–46. Successors to Wood and Caldwell.
Impressed. Other self-explanatory name marks also used.

Appendix

APPENDIX

Registration Marks
1842–1883

A diamond-shaped mark, printed or impressed, is often seen on wares first made between 1842 and 1883, indicating that to prevent piracy a particular design of article had been registered with the London Patent Office. It will of course be clear that the information thus given in the marks will only indicate the earliest possible date of manufacture, since the design so registered could have been continued in succeeding years.

Year Letters in top angle of diamond
1842–67

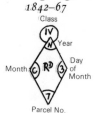

A 1845	G 1863	M 1859	S 1849	Y 1853
B 1858	H 1843	N 1864	T 1867	Z 1860
C 1844	I 1846	O 1862	U 1848	
D 1852	J 1854	P 1851	V 1850	
E 1855	K 1857	Q 1866	W 1865	
F 1847	L 1856	R 1861	X 1842	

Year Letters in right-hand angle of diamond
1868–83

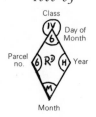

A 1871	H 1869	P 1877	X 1868
C 1870	I 1872	S 1875	Y 1879
D 1878	J 1880	U 1874	
E 1881	K 1883	V 1876	
F 1873	L 1882	W 1878	

Month Letters – the same for both arrangements

A – December	H – April
B – October	I – July
C or O – January	K – Nov. and Dec. 1860
D – September	M – June
E – May	R – August, and Sept. 1–19, 1857
G – February	W – March

Registration Numbers
from 1884

Numbers prefixed 'Rd.' or 'Rd. No.' are found on many wares made from January 1884 onwards, of which a full list may be found in G. A. Godden's 'Encyclopaedia' of marks, pages 527–8.

Minton Year Cyphers

Much Minton ware may be identified and dated by the presence thereon of impressed year cyphers which were introduced in 1842.

1842	1843	1844	1845	1846
✳	△	▢	✕	⬭
1847	1848	1849	1850	1851
⌒	⊷	⋈	♧	∴
1852	1853	1854	1855	1856
∨	☙	℅	✳	φ
1857	1858	1859	1860	1861
◇	⅁	⚐	♋	⋏
1862	1863	1864	1865	1866
⚥	⍭	⋝	〰	⤫

Minton Year Cyphers

1867	1868	1869	1870	1871

1872	1873	1874	1875	1876

1877	1878	1879	1880	1881

1882	1883	1884	1885	1886

1887	1888	1889	1890	1891

1892	1893	1894	1895	1896

1897	1898	1899	1900	1901

1902	1903	1904	1905	1906

1907	1908	1909	1910	1911

1912	1913	1914	1915	1916

1917	1918	1919	1920	1921

Minton Year Cyphers

1922	1923	1924	1925	1926
ᴨᴵᴵᴵᴴ	╫	卐	☆	ᴍ

1927	1928	1929	1930	1931
卍	⬡	Ж	⚥	♠

1932	1933	1934	1935	1936
쌜	Λ	❖	☼	♋

1937	1938	1939	1940	1941
◉	✠	⛵	☜	✈

1942				
V				

The Royal Arms Mark

Many printed marks upon 19th and 20th century wares incorporate a version of the Royal Arms, often with self-explanatory names and place-names. In their absence, it is difficult to attribute origin, though the actual form of the Arms themselves provides a clue as to date of manufacture. Thus, before 1837 we find an extra tiny shield in the centre which is missing in later versions. Among those potters who made use of the Royal Arms as factory marks are the following, with dates:

William & Thos. Adams, 1866–92

W. Adams & Sons, 1890–1914

Samuel Alcock & Co., *c.* 1828–59

Birks Bros. & Seddon, 1878–86

Brown-Westhead Moore & Co., 1890–1904

Henry Burgess, 1864–92

Clementson Bros. Ltd., 1867–80

R. Cochran & Co., 1846–1918

Cochran & Fleming, 1900–20

The Royal Arms Mark

Cockson & Seddon, 1875–77

Elsmore & Forster, 1853–71

Ford, Challinor & Co., 1865–80

Jacob & Thos. Furnival, *c.* 1845

Thos. Furnival & Sons, 1818–90

Hallam & Day, 1880–85

C. & W. K. Harvey, 1835–53

Hicks & Meigh, *c.* 1806–22

Hicks, Meigh & Johnson, 1822–35

Johnson Bros. (Hanley) Ltd., 1883–1913

James Kent Ltd., 1897–1915

John Matthews, 1870–88

Alfred Meakin Ltd., *c.* 1897–1910

Charles Meakin, 1883–89

Henry Meakin, 1873–76

J. & G. Meakin, *c.* 1890

Charles Meigh & Son, 1851–61

Mellor, Taylor & Co., 1880–1904

Morley & Ashworth, 1859–62

Pinder, Bourne & Co., 1862–82

Plymouth Pottery Co., 1856–63

F. Primavesi & Son, *c.* 1850–1915

John Ridway & Co., *c.* 1830–55

G. W. Turner & Sons, 1891–95

Edward Walley, 1845–56

Arthur J. Wilkinson Ltd., *c.* 1885–1900

Wood & Sons Ltd., *c.* 1910

The Staffordshire Knot Mark

Many firms in the Potteries used the 'Staffordshire Knot' as a mark usually with distinguishing initials in the three loops, as follows:

H. Aynsley & Co., H.A. & Co., 1873–1932

Badley & Co., B. & Co., 1865

Geo. Frederick Bowers, G.F.B., 1842–68

Burslem School of Art, B.S.A., 1935–41

Goodwin & Bullock, G. & B., 1852–6

Thomas Green, FENTON, T.G., (with crown), 1847–59

T. A. & S. Green, TA & SG, (with crown), 1876–89

Hanley Porcelain Company, H.P. Co., 1892–9

Arthur J. Mountford, A.J.M., 1897–1901

George Phillips, Name in full, *c.* 1834–48

Ridgway, Sparks & Ridgway, R.S.R., 1873–9

Robinson & Son, R. & S., *c.* 1881–1903

The Staffordshire Knot Mark

Smith & Binnall, S. & B.T., 1897–1900
Thomas Twyford, T.T.H., 1860–98
Wellington Pottery Co., W.P.Co., *c.* 1899–1901
Wilkinson & Wardle, W.W., *c.* 1864–66
H. J. Wood, Ltd., H.J.W.B., *c.* 1884
W. Wood & Co., W. & W. Co., 1880–1915.

Pilkington's Tile & Pottery Co. Ltd.
Clifton Junction, Nr. Manchester
c. 1897–1938 and 1948–57

Many potters have tried to emulate the lovely coloured
glazes of the Orientals, among them William De Morgan,
Bernard Moore, W. Howson Taylor (Ruskin Pottery) and
William and Joseph Burton of Pilkingtons and the Royal
Lancastrian Pottery. At the beginning of the present century
the firm was probably the largest manufactory of artistic
decorative tiles in the country, specialising in beautiful
lustre effects. Since many items were designed by craftsmen
of note, we give the marks usually found on examples of
their work.

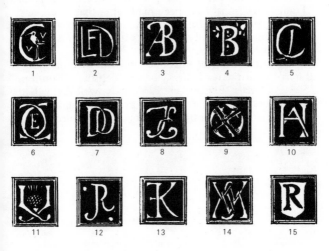

Wedgwood Year Letters
Period 1860–1906

From 1860 onwards earthenwares bear impressed three letter year marks, the last letter denoting the year of manufacture. Thus, O–1860 to Z–1871, A–1872 to Z–1897, A–1898 to I–1906. This repetition may obviously cause some confusion, somewhat eased by the appearance of the word ENGLAND from 1891 onwards. These year marks are accompanied by the standard impressed WEDGWOOD factory mark.

Approximate Dating by Means of Marks

Apart from the fact that many marks were used only during some specific period, there are other factors which help in the approximate dating of a marked piece. These are as follows:

1. To comply with the American McKinley Tariff Act, the word 'ENGLAND' was added to marks from 1891.
2. 'Made in England' signifies a 20th century origin.
3. The introduction of the Trade Mark Act of 1862 ensures that any piece bearing a mark which incorporates 'Trade Mark' must have been made after that date.
4. Not until the 19th century, when printed marks became more generally used, was it common practice to include pattern names in them.
5. Since the dates of introduction of new, usually more durable or attractive bodies, such as 'Feltspar', 'Ironstone', 'Stone China', 'Regent' etc. are fairly well-defined, the inclusion of such names in marks gives a fair indication of approximate date of earliest possible manufacture.

Selected Initial Marks

The following marks have been selected from a very large number as being those most likely to be found either alone or incorporated into factory or pattern marks. For the most part they are printed, and their presence usually indicates that the piece under examination is of 19th century manufacture. The mark having been identified, further details of the factory should be looked up in a more comprehensive and detailed reference book, such as G. A. Godden's 'Encyclopaedia of Pottery and Porcelain Marks'.

In alphabetical order

A. & B.	Adams & Bromley	Hanley	1873–86
A. & C.	Adams & Cooper	Longton	1850–77
A. & Co.	Edward Asbury & Co.	Longton	1875–1925
B.	John & Edward Baddeley	Shelton	1874–1806
B. & B.	Blackhurst & Bourne	Burslem	1880–92
B.B. & Co.	Glamorgan Pottery	Swansea	1813–38
B.B. & I.	Glamorgan Pottery	Swansea	1813–38
B.B.W. & M.	Bates, Brown Westhead & Moore	Shelton	1859–61
B. & C.	Bridgwood & Clarke	Burslem	1857–64
B.G. & W.	Bates, Gildea & Walker	Burslem	1878–81
B.H. & Co.	Beech Hancock & Co.	Burslem	1851–5
B. & M.	Bagshaw & Meir	Burslem	1802–6
B.P. Co.	Brownhills Pottery Co.	Tunstall	1872–96
B. & S.	Bishop & Stonier	Hanley	1891–1910
B. & S.H.	Benjamin & Sampson Hancock	Stoke	1876–81
B.S. & T.	Barker, Sutton & Till	Burslem	1834–43
B.W.M.	Brown Westhead Moors & Co.	Hanley	1862–1904
C.A. & Sons	Charles Allerton & Sons	Longton	*c.* 1890–1942
C. & D.	Cooper & Dethick	Longton	1876–88
C. & E.	Corke & Edge	Burslem	1846–60
C. & F.	Cochran & Cleming	Glasgow	1896
C. & G.	Copeland & Garrett	Stoke	*c.* 1833–47
C.H.	Charles Hobson	Burslem	1865–80
C.H. & S.	Charles Hobson	Burslem	1865–80
C.J.M. & Co.	Charles James Mason	Lane Delph	1829–45
C.K.	Charles Keeling	Shelton	1822–5

(contd.)

C. & M.	Clokie & Masterman	Castleford	1872–87
C.M.	Charles Meigh	Hanley	1835–49
C.M. & S.	Charles Meigh & Son	Hanley	1851–61
C.P. Co.	Clyde Pottery Co.	Greenock	*c.* 1815–1903
C. & R.	Chesworth & Robinson	Lane End	1825–40
C. & R.	Chetham & Robinson	Longton	1822–37
C.T.M.	C. T. Maling	Newcastle	*c.* 1859–90
D. & Co.	Cambrian Pottery	Swansea	*c.* 1811–17
D.B. & Co.	Davenport Banks & Co.	Hanley	1860–73
D.B. & Co.	Davenport Beck & Co.	Hanley	1873–80
D.B. & Co.	Dunn Bennett & Co.	Burslem	1875–1907
D.D. & Co.	David Dunderdale & Co.	Castleford	1790–1820
D.L. & Co.	David Lockhart & Co.	Glasgow	1865–98
E. & B.	Edwards & Brown	Longton	1882–1910
E. & G.P.	Edward & Geo. Phillips	Longport	1822–34
E.K.B.	Elkin, Knight & Bridgwood	Fenton	1827–40
E.M. & Co.	Edge Malkin & Co.	Burslem	1871–1900
E.W. & S.	Enoch Wood & Sons	Burslem	*c.* 1818–46
F. & Co.	Thomas Fell & Co.	Newcastle	1830–90
F.D.	Francis Dillon	Cobridge	*c.* 1834–43
F. & R.	Ford & Riley	Burslem	1882–93
F. & R.P.	F. & R. Pratt & Co.	Fenton	*c.* 1818–60
F.W. & Co.	F. Winkle & Co.	Stoke	1890–1910
G. & C.J.M.	G. M. & C. J. Mason	Lane Delph	1813–29
G.C.P. Co.	Clyde Pottery Co.	Greenock	*c.* 1815–1903
G.D.	Guest & Dewsbury	Llanelly	1877–1927
G. & D.L.	Guest & Dewsbury	Llanelly	1877–1927
G.G. & Co.	George Grainger & Co.	Worcester	1848–60
G.G.W.	George Grainger & Co.	Worcester	1848–60
G.L.A. & Bros.	G. L. Ashworth & Bros.	Hanley	1862–90
G.P. & Co.	Glamorgan Pottery	Swansea	1813–38
G.P. Co.	Clyde Pottery Co.	Greenock	*c.* 1815–1903
G.S. & Co.	George Skinner & Co.	Stockton	1855–70
G.S. & S.	George Shaw & Sons	Rotherham	1887–1948
G.T. & S.	G. W. Turner & Sons	Tunstall	1873–95
G.W.	George Grainger & Co.	Worcester	1848–60
G.W.	Geo. Warrilow	Longton	1887–92
G. & W.	Gildea & Walker	Burslem	1881–5

(contd.)

G.W.T.S.	G. W. Turner & Sons	Tunstall	1873–95
G.W.T. & S.	G. W. Turner & Sons	Tunstall	1873–95
H. & Co.	Hackwood & Co.	Hanley	1807–27
H.A. & Co.	Harvey Adams & Co.	Longton	1870–85
H.A. & Co.	Henry Alcock & Co.	Cobridge	1861–80
H.A. & Co.	H. Aynsley & Co.	Longton	1873–1932
H. & C.	Hope & Carter	Burslem	1862–80
H.M.J.	Hicks, Meigh & Johnson	Shelton	1822–35
H.P. & M.	Holmes, Plant & Maydew	Burslem	1876–85
I.E.B.	John & Edward Baddeley	Shelton	1784–1806
I.W. & Co.	Isaac Wilson & Co.	Middlesbrough	1852–87
J.B.	J. & M. P. Bell & Co.	Glasgow	1842–70
J.B.	James Broadhurst & Sons	Fenton	1862–70
J.B. & Co.	J. Bennett & Co.	Hanley	1896–1900
J.B. & S.	James Broadhurst & Sons	Fenton	1870–1922
J.B.W.	James B. Wathen	Fenton	1864–9
J.C.	Joseph Clementson	Shelton	1839–64
J. & C.W.	James & Charles Wileman	Fenton	*c.* 1864–97
J.D. & Co.	J. Dimmock & Co.	Hanley	1862–78
J.E.	John Edwards & Co.	Fenton	1847–73
J.E. & Co.	John Edwards & Co.	Fenton	1847–73
J. & G.A.	John & George Alcock	Cobridge	1839–46
J.H. & Co.	Joseph Heath & Co.	Tunstall	1828–41
J.L.C.	Jonathan Lowe Chetham	Longton	1841–62
J.M.	John Mayer	Foley	1833–41
J.M.	John Meir	Tunstall	1812–36
J.M. & Co.	North British Pottery	Glasgow	1869–75
J. & M. P. B. & Co.	J. & M. P. Bell & Co.	Glasgow	1842–70
J.M. & S.	John Meir & Son	Tunstall	1837–97
J. & P.	Jackson & Patterson	Newcastle	1830–45
J.R.	James Reeves	Fenton	1870
J.R.	John Ridgway	Hanley	1830–41
J.R.	Joseph Robinson	Burslem	1876–98
J.R. & Co.	Coalport Porcelain Works	Coalport	1850–70

(contd.)

J.R. & Co.	John Ridgway & Co.	Hanley	1841–55
J. & R.G.	John & Robert Godwin	Cobridge	1834–66
J.R.H.	J. & R. Hammersley	Hanley	1877–1917
J.S. & Co.	J. Shore & Co.	Longton	1887–190s
J. & T.E.	James & Thos. Edwards	Burslem	1839–41
J.V.	James Vernon & Son	Burslem	1860–74
J.W. & Co.	J. Wileman & Co.	Fenton	*c.* 1864–9
J.W.P.	J. W. Pankhurst & Co.	Hanley	1850–82
J.W.R.	John and William Ridgway	Hanley	1814–30
J. & W.R.	John and William Ridgway	Hanley	1814–30
J.Y.	John Yates	Hanley	*c.* 1784–1835
K. & Co.	Keeling & Co.	Burslem	1886–1936
K.E. & B.	Knight Elkin & Bridgwood	Fenton	1830–40
K.E. & Co.	Knight Elkin & Co.	Fenton	1826–46
K. & M.	Keys & Mountford	Stoke	1850–7
L.E. & S.	Liddle, Elliot & Son	Longport	1862–71
L. & H.	Lockett & Hulme	Lane End	1822–6
L.P. & Co.	Livesley Powell & Co.	Hanley	1851–66
M. & A.	Morley & Ashworth	Hanley	1859–62
M.E. & Co.	Middlesbrough Earthenware Co.	Middlesbrough	1844–52
M.P. Co.	Middlesbrough Pottery Co.	Middlesbrough	1834–44
M. & S.	Maddock & Seddon	Burslem	1839–42
M.W. & Co.	Morgan Wood & Co.	Burslem	1860–70
N.W.P. Co.	New Wharf Pottery Co.	Burslem	1874–98
O.H.E.C.	Old Hall Earthenware Co. Ltd.	Hanley	1861–1886
P. & A.	Pountney & Allies	Bristol	1816–35
P. & B.	Powell & Bishop	Hanley	1876–8
P.B. & H.	Pinder, Bourne & Hope	Burslem	1851–62
P.B. & S.	Powell, Bishop & Stoner	Hanley	1878–91
P. & Co.	Pountney & Co.	Bristol	1849–89
P. & S.	Pratt & Simpson	Fenton	1878–83

(contd.)

P.W. & Co.	Podmore, Walker & Co.	Tunstall	1834–59
R.B.	Robinson Brothers	Castleford	1807–1904
R.C. & Co.	R. Cochran & Co.	Glasgow	1846–1918
R.G.S.	R. G. Scrivener & Co.	Hanley	1870–83
R. & M.	Ridgway & Morley	Hanley	1842–44
R.M.A.	R. M. Astbury	Shelton	late 18th cent.
R.M.W. & Co.	Ridgway, Morley Wear & Co.	Hanley	1836–42
R. & P.	Rhodes & Proctor	Burslem	1883–5
R.S.A.	Ridgway, Sparks & Ridgway	Hanley	1873–9
R.S. & S.	Ralph Stevenson & Son	Cobridge	c. 1831–35
R. & T.	Reed & Taylor	Ferrybridge	1820–56
R. & W.	Robinson & Wood	Hanley	1832–6
R.W. & B.	Robinson, Wood & Brownfield	Cobridge	1838–41
S. & Co.	Isleworth Pottery	Isleworth	c. 1750–1825
S. & Sons	Southwick Pottery	Sunderland	c. 1829–38
S.B. & Co.	Southwick Pottery	Sunderland	c. 1838–54
S. & G.	Isleworth Pottery	Isleworth	c. 1750–1825
S.K. & Co.	Samuel Keeling & Co.	Hanley	1840–50
S. & S.	Southwick Pottery	Sunderland	c. 1872–82
S.W.P.	South Wales Pottery	Llanelly	c. 1839–58
T. & B.	Tomkinson & Billington	Longton	1868–70
T.B. & Co.	Thomas Booth & Co.	Burslem & Tunstall	1868–72
T.B. & S.	Thomas Booth & Son	Tunstall	1872–6
T. & B.G.	Thos. & Benjamin Godwin	Burslem	1809–34
T. & C.F.	T. & C. Ford	Hanley	1854–71
T.F. & Co.	Thomas Fell & Co.	Newcastle	1830–90
T.F. & Co.	Thomas Furnival & Co.	Hanley	c. 1844–6
T.H. & P.	Turner, Hassall & Peake	Stoke	1865–9
T. & L.	Tams & Lowe	Longton	1865–74
T.R. & P.	Tundley, Rhodes & Proctor	Burslem	1878–83
T.S. & C.	Thos. Shirley & Co.	Greenock	1840–57
T.T.	Taylor, Tunnicliffe & Co.	Hanley	c. 1868–80

(contd.)

T. & T.	Turner & Tomkinson	Tunstall	1860–72
T.T. & Co.	Taylor, Tunnicliffe & Co.	Hanley	*c.* 1868–80
T.W. & Co.	Thomas C. Wild & Co.	Longton	*c.* 1896–1904
T.W. & Co.	Thomas Wood & Co.	Burslem	1885–96
U.H. & W.	Unwin, Holmes & Worthington	Hanley	*c.* 1865–8
W.A. & Co.	A. Adams & Sons	Tunstall & Stoke	1893–1917
W.A. & S.	A. Adams & Sons	Tunstall & Stoke	1819–64
W.A.A.	W. A. Adderley	Longton	1876–85
W.A.A. & Co.	W. A. Adderley	Longton	1886–1905
W.B.	William Brownfield	Cobridge	1850–71
W. & B.	Wood & Baggaley	Burslem	1870–80
W. & B.	Wood & Brownfield	Cobridge	*c.* 1838–50
W.B. & S.	William Brownfield & Sons	Cobridge	after 1871
W.B. & Son	William Brownfield & Sons	Cobridge	after 1871
W. & C.	Walker & Carter	Longton	1866–89
W. & C.	Wood & Challinor	Tunstall	1828–43
W. & Co.	Wade & Co.	Burslem	1887–1927
W.C. & Co.	Wood, Challinor & Co.	Tunstall	*c.* 1860–4
W.E.W.	W. E. Withinshaw	Burslem	1873–8
W.F. & Co.	Whittingham, Ford & Co.	Burslem	1868–73
W.F. & R.	Whittingham, Ford & Riley	Burslem	1876–82
W. & H.	Worthington & Harrop	Hanley	*c.* 1784–1835
W.H. & Co.	Whittaker, Heath & Co.	Hanley	1892–8
W.H.G.	William Henry Goss	Stoke	*c.* 1862
W. & J.H.	W. & J. Harding	Shelton	1862–72
W.R.	William Ridgway	Hanley	1830–40
W.R. & Co.	William Ridgway & Co.	Hanley	1834–54
W.R.S. & Co.	William Ridgway & Co.	Hanley	1838–48
W.S. & Co.	William Smith & Co.	Stockton	1825–55
W.W. & Co.	W. Wood & Co.	Burslem	1873–1932

Selected Initial Marks

In alphabetical order of factories

A. & B.	Adams & Bromley	Hanley	1873–86
A. & C.	Adams & Cooper	Longton	1850–77
H.A. & CO.	Harvey Adams & Co.	Longton	1870–85
W.A. & S.	A. Adams & Sons	Tunstall & Stoke	1819–64
W.A. & CO.	A. Adams & Sons	Tunstall & Stoke	1893–1917
W.A.A.	W. A. Adderley	Longton	1876–85
W.A.A. & CO.	W. A. Adderley	Longton	1886–1905
H.A. & CO.	Henry Alcock & Co.	Cobridge	1861–80
J. & G.A.	John & George Alcock	Cobridge	1839–46
C.A. & SONS	Charles Allerton & Sons	Longton	*c.* 1890–1942
A. & CO.	Edward Asbury & Co.	Longton	1875–1925
G.L.A. & BROS.	G. L. Ashworth & Bros.	Hanley	1862–90
R.M.A.	R. M. Astbury	Shelton	Late 18th cent.
H.A. & CO.	H. Aynsley & Co.	Longton	1873–1932
B. or I.E.B.	John & Edward Baddeley	Shelton	1784–1806
B. & M.	Bagshaw & Meir	Burslem	1802–8
B.B. & I. ⎫ B.B. & CO. ⎬ G.P. CO. ⎭	Glamorgan Pottery	Swansea	1813–38
B.S. & T.	Barker, Sutton & Till	Burslem	1834–43
B.B.W. & M.	Bates, Brown Westhead & Moore	Shelton	1859–61
B.G. & W.	Bates, Gildea & Walker	Burslem	1878–81
B.H. & CO.	Beech Hancock & Co.	Burslem	1851–5
J.B. ⎫ J. & M.P.B. ⎬ & CO. ⎭	J. & M. P. Bell & Co.	Glasgow	1842–70
J.B. & CO.	J. Bennett & Co.	Hanley	1896–1900
B. & S.	Bishop & Stonier	Hanley	1891–1910
B. & B.	Blackhurst & Bourne	Burslem	1880–92
T.B. & CO.	Thomas Booth & Co.	Burslem & Tunstall	1868–72
T.B. & S.	Thomas Booth & Son	Tunstall	1872–6
B. & C.	Bridgwood & Clarke	Burslem	1857–64
J.B.	James Broadhurst & Sons	Fenton	1862–70

(contd.)

J.B. & S.	James Broadhurst & Sons	Fenton	1870–1922
W.B.	William Brownfield	Cobridge	1850–71
W.B. & S. (or Son)	William Brownfield & Sons	Cobridge	After 1871
B.P. CO.	Brownhills Pottery Co.	Tunstall	1872–96
B.W.M.	Brown Westhead, Moore & Co.	Hanley	1862–1904
C. & R.	Chesworth & Robinson	Lane End	1825–40
J.L.C.	Jonathan Lowe Chetham	Longton	1841–62
C. & R.	Chetham & Robinson	Longton	1822–37
J.C.	Joseph Clementson	Shelton	1839–64
C. & M.	Clokie & Masterman	Castleford	1872–87
G.C.P. CO. C.P. CO. G.P.CO.	Clyde Pottery Co.	Greenock	*c.* 1815–1903
J.R. & CO.	Coalport Porcelain Works	Coalport	1850–70
R.C. & CO.	R. Cochran & Co.	Glasgow	1846–1918
C. & F.	Cochran & Fleming	Glasgow	1896 onwards
C. & D.	Cooper & Dethick	Longton	1876–88
C. & G.	Copeland & Garrett	Stoke	*c.* 1833–47
C. & E.	Cork & Edge	Burslem	1846–60
D.B. & CO.	Davenport Banks & Co.	Hanley	1860–73
	Davenport Beck & Co.	Hanley	1873–80
F.D.	Francis Dillon	Cobridge	*c.* 1834–43
J.D. & CO.	J. Dimmock & Co.	Hanley	1862–78
D.D. & CO.	David Dunderdale & Co.	Castleford	1790–1820
D.B. & CO.	Dunn Bennett & Co.	Burslem	1875–1907
E.M. & CO.	Edge Malkin & Co.	Burslem	1871–1900
J.E. or J.E. & CO.	John Edwards & Co.	Fenton	1847–73
J. & T.E.	James & Thos. Edwards	Burslem	1839–41
E. & B.	Edwards & Brown	Longton	1882–1910
E.K.B.	Elkin, Knight & Bridgwood	Fenton	1827–40
L.E. & S.	Liddle, Elliot & Son	Longport	1862–71
F. & CO. T.F. & CO.	Thomas Fell & Co.	Newcastle	1830–90
F. & R.	Ford & Riley	Burslem	1882–93

contd.)

T. & C.F.	T. & C. Ford	Hanley	1854–71
T.F. & CO.	Thomas Furnival & Co.	Hanley	c. 1844–6
G. & W.	Gildea & Walker	Burslem	1881–5
J. & R.G.	John & Robert Godwin	Cobridge	1834–66
T. & B.G.	Thos. & Benjamin Godwin	Burslem	1809–34
W.H.G.	William Henry Goss	Stoke	c. 1862 on
G.G. & CO. G.G.W. G.W.	George Grainger & Co.	Worcester	1848–60
G. & D.L. G.D.	Guest & Dewsbury	Llanelly	1877–1927
H. & CO.	Hackwood & Co.	Hanley	1807–27
J.R.H.	J. & R. Hammersley	Hanley	1877–1917
B. & S.H.	Benjamin & Sampson Hancock	Stoke	1876–81
W. & J.H.	W. & J. Harding	Shelton	1862–72
J.H. & CO.	Joseph Heath & Co.	Tunstall	1828–41
H.M.J.	Hicks, Meigh & Johnson	Shelton	1822–35
C.H. or C.H. & S.	Charles Hobson	Burslem	1865–80
H.P. & M.	Holmes, Plant & Maydew	Burslem	1876–85
H. & C.	Hope & Carter	Burslem	1862–80
S. & CO. S. & G.	Isleworth Pottery	Isleworth	c. 1750–1825
J. & P.	Jackson & Patterson	Newcastle	1830–45
C.K.	Charles Keeling	Shelton	1822–5
K. & CO.	Keeling & Co.	Burslem	1886–1936
S.K. & CO.	Samuel Keeling & Co.	Hanley	1840–50
K. & M.	Keys & Mountford	Stoke	1850–7
W.K. & CO.	William Kirkby & Co.	Fenton	1879–85
K.E. & CO.	Knight Elkin & Co.	Fenton	1826–46
K.E. & B.	Knight Elkin & Bridgwood	Fenton	1830–40
L.P. & CO.	Livesley Powell & Co.	Hanley	1851–66
L. & H.	Lockett & Hulme	Lane End	1822–6
D.L. & CO.	David Lockhart & Co.	Glasgow	1865–98
M. & S.	Maddock & Seddon	Burslem	1839–42
C.T.M.	C. T. Maling	Newcastle	c. 1859–90
C.J.M. & CO.	Charles James Mason	Lane Delph	1829–45
G. & C.J.M.	G. M. & C. J. Mason	Lane Delph	1813–29
J.M.	John Mayer	Foley	1833–41
C.M.	Charles Meigh	Hanley	1835–49
C.M. & S.	Charles Meigh & Son	Hanley	1851–61

(contd.)

J.M.	John Meir	Tunstall	1812–36
J.M. & S.	John Meir & Son	Tunstall	1837–97
M.E. & CO.	Middlesborough Earthenware Co.	Middlesborough	1844–52
M.P. CO.	Middlesborough Pottery Co.	Middlesborough	1834–44
M.W. & CO.	Morgan Wood & Co.	Burslem	1860–70
M. & A.	Morley & Ashworth	Hanley	1859–62
N.W.P. CO.	New Wharf Pottery Co.	Burslem	1878–94
J.M. & CO.	North British Pottery	Glasgow	1869–75
O.H.E.C.	Old Hall Earthenware Co. Ltd.	Hanley	1861–188
J.W.P.	J. W. Pankhurst & Co.	Hanley	1850–82
E. & G.P.	Edward & Geo. Phillips	Longport	1822–34
P.B. & H.	Pinder, Bourne & Hope	Burslem	1851–62
P.W. & CO.	Podmore, Walker & Co.	Tunstall	1834–59
P. & CO.	Pountney & Co.	Bristol	1849–89
P. & A.	Pountney & Allies	Bristol	1816–35
P. & B.	Powell & Bishop	Hanley	1876–8
P.B. & S.	Powell, Bishop & Stoner	Hanley	1878–91
F. & R.P.	F. & R. Pratt & Co.	Fenton	*c.* 1818–60
P. & S.	Pratt & Simpson	Fenton	1878–83
R. & T.	Reed & Taylor	Ferrybridge	1820–56
J.R.	James Reeves	Fenton	1870 on
R. & P.	Rhodes & Proctor	Burslem	1883–5
J.R.	John Ridgway	Hanley	1830–41
J.R. & CO.	John Ridgway & Co.	Hanley	1841–55
J.W.R. / J. & W.R.	John and William Ridgway	Hanley	1814–30
R.M.W. & CO.	Ridgway, Morley, Wear & Co.	Hanley	1836–42
R. & M.	Ridgway & Morley	Hanley	1842–44
R.S.R.	Ridgway, Sparks & Ridgway	Hanley	1873–9
W.R.	William Ridgway	Hanley	1830–40
W.R. & CO.	William Ridgway & Co.	Hanley	1834–54
W.R.S. & CO.	William Ridgway, Son & Co.	Hanley	1838–48
R.B.	Robinson Brothers	Castleford	1897–190
J.R.	Joseph Robinson	Burslem	1876–98
R. & W.	Robinson & Wood	Hanley	1832–6

(*contd.*)

R.W. & B.	Robinson, Wood & Brownfield	Cobridge	1838–41
R.G.S.	R. G. Scrivener & Co.	Hanley	1870–83
G.S. & S.	George Shaw & Sons	Rotherham	1887–1948
T.S. & C.	Thos. Shirley & Co.	Greenock	1840–57
J.S. & CO.	J. Shore & Co.	Longton	1887–1905
G.S. & CO.	George Skinner & Co.	Stockton	1855–70
W.S. & CO.	William Smith & Co.	Stockton	1825–55
S.W.P.	South Wales Pottery	Llanelly	c. 1839–58
S. & SONS	Southwick Pottery	Sunderland	c. 1829–38
S.B. & CO.	Southwick Pottery	Sunderland	c. 1838–54
S. & S.	Southwick Pottery	Sunderland	c. 1872–82
R.S. & S.	Ralph Stevenson & Son	Cobridge	c. 1832–35
D. & CO.	Cambrian Pottery	Swansea	c. 1811–17
T. & L.	Tams & Lowe	Longton	1865–74
T.T. T.T. & CO. }	Taylor, Tunnicliffe & Co.	Hanley	c. 1868–80
T. & B.	Tomkinson & Billington	Longton	1868–70
T.R. & P.	Tundley, Rhodes & Proctor	Burslem	1873–83
G.W.T.S. G.W.T. & S. }	G. W. Turner & Sons	Tunstall	1873–95
G.T. & S. T.H. & P. }	Turner, Hassall & Peake	Stoke	1865–9
T. & T.	Turner & Tomkinson	Tunstall	1860–72
U.H. & W.	Unwin, Holmes & Worthington	Hanley	c. 1865–8
J.V.	James Vernon & Son	Burslem	1860–74
W. & CO.	Wade & Co.	Burslem	1887–1927
W. & C.	Walker & Carter	Longton	1866–89
G.W.	Geo. Warrilow	Longton	1887–92
J.B.W.	James B. Wathen	Fenton	1864–9
W.H. & CO.	Whittaker, Heath & Co.	Hanley	1892–8
W.F. & CO.	Whittingham, Ford & Co.	Burslem	1868–73
W.F. & R.	Whittingham, Ford & Riley	Burslem	1876–82
T.W. & CO.	Thos. C. Wild & Co.	Longton	c. 1896–1904
J. & C.W.	James & Charles Wileman	Fenton	c. 1864–97
J.W. & CO.	J. Wileman & Co.	Fenton	c. 1864–9
I.W. & CO.	Isaac Wilson & Co.	Middlesborough	1852–87

(contd.)

F.W. & CO.	F. Winkle & Co.	Stoke	1890–1910
W.E.W.	W. E. Withinshaw	Burslem	1873–8
W. & B.	Wood & Baggaley	Burslem	1870–80
	Wood & Brownfield	Cobridge	c. 1838–50
W. & C.	Wood & Challinor	Tunstall	1828–43
W.C. & CO.	Wood, Challinor & Co.	Tunstall	c. 1860–4
E.W. & S.	Enoch Wood & Sons	Burslem	c. 1818–46
T.W. & CO.	Thomas Wood & Co.	Burslem	1885–96
W.W. & CO.	W. Wood & Co.	Burslem	1873–1932
W. & H.	Worthington & Harrop	Hanley	1856–73
J.Y.	John Yates	Hanley	c. 1784–1835

BIBLIOGRAPHY

The books listed here are specialised, giving only such incidental information concerning the wares themselves as is necessary for the purposes of identification and dating.

'Encyclopaedia of British Pottery and Porcelain Marks', G. A. Godden, 1964

'An Illustrated Encyclopaedia of British Pottery and Porcelain', G. A. Godden, 1966.

'A Dictionary of Marks, Pottery and Porcelain', R. M. and T. H. Kovel, 1953.

'English China and its Marks', T. H. Ormslee, 1959.

'Marks and Monograms', W. Chaffers. 15th edition, 1964.

'Handbook of Old Pottery and Porcelain Marks', C. Jordan Thorn, 1947.

'Handbook of Pottery and Porcelain Marks', J. P. Cushion and W. B. Honey, 1962.

'British Pottery Marks', G. Woolliscroft Rhead, 1910.

Marks Containing Initials

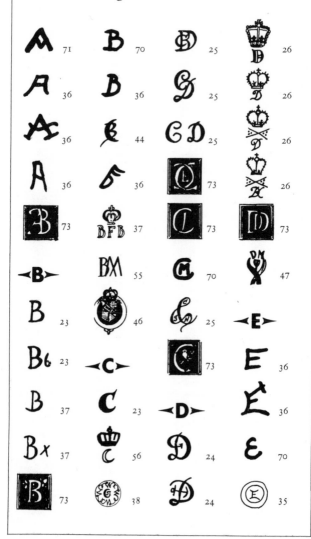

Marks Containing Initials (cont'd)

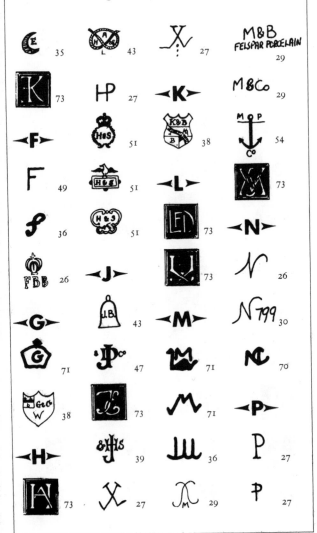

89

Marks Containing Initials (cont'd)

Ᵽ 36	𝓢 70	T° 22	[W] 35
℗ 36	S 23	T° 31	⋁ 35
𝓹 36	(S H D mark) 26	(TLV monogram) 62	W 27
P98 31	So 23	(TR&Cº) 57	⋙ 69
P. & A. 45	Sₓ 23	◄V►	w 36
P. & CO. 44	◄T►	V 71	ᴄ 36
◄R►	T 22	✓ 36	(WMS mark) 42
R 36	T 70	V 69	◄X►
R 73	T 36	◄W►	X 23
R 73	T 36	W 35	(square mark) 73
◄S►	ℛ 36	ℊℊ 35	

Marks Containing Initials (cont'd)

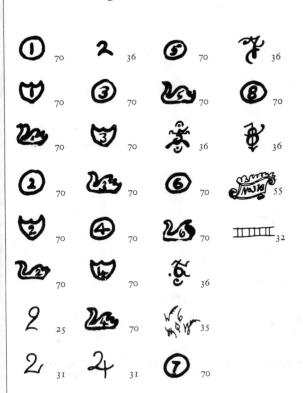

Y 36 λ 69 ⋖Z⋗ Z 69

Marks Containing Numerals

① 70 2 36 ⑤ 70 𝒴 36

♈ 70 ③ 70 𝓤𝒻 70 ⑧ 70

𝓤𝓪 70 ♥3 70 🐜 36 𝓫 36

② 70 𝓤𝓼 70 ⑥ 70 No316 55

♈2 70 ④ 70 𝓤6 70 ▭▭▭ 32

𝓤2 70 ♥17 70 6 36

2 25 𝓤4 70 W6 35

2 31 2ꝗ 31 ⑦ 70

Marks Containing Words

47

47

E

B

47

D. J. EVANS & CO. 62

58

COALBROOKDALE 25

F

26

61

29

BRAMELD 58

COPELAND 33

FENTON STONE WORKS 54

BRISTOL 28

33

FLIGHT 37

C

60

Flight 37

CAMBRIA 62

CAMBRIAN 62

Flight. 37

Chamberlains 38

D

Flight & Barr 37

CHAMBERLAINS 38

C Dale 25

G

38

DILLWYN & CO. 33

29

Marks Containing Words (cont'd)

George Grainger
Royal China Works
Worcester 38

 27

POUNTNEY & ALLIES ✝ 45

Grainger Lee & Co.
Worcester 38

HARTLEY, GREENS
& CO. 52

POUNTNEY & CO.
44

GRESLEY 50

◄N►

◄S►

◄H►

NEALE & WILSON
56

Salopian 23

Hadley 39

◄O►

50

R Hancock fecit 36

 29

◄W►

HERCULANEUM 27

◄P►

WILSON 56

Pictorial Marks

🌙 36   🌙 22   🌙 35   ⚔ 25

🌙 28   🌙 35   ⚔ 23   ⚔ 28

🌙* 31   🌙 35   ⚔ 23   ⚔ 62

Pictorial Marks (cont'd)

35	49	42	70
35	22	43	70
35	46	45	71
22	24	44	71
70	24	33	71
26	46	56	71
22	24	50	71
24	63	35	71
24	42	69	71
36	70	70	
24	27	70	

Hieroglyphics

Square devices

 69   70   70   70

 70   70   71   71

Angular devices

 69   70   69   36

 70   36   69   36

 70   36   71   36

 70   70   71

 70   69   71

 70   36   71

Round devices

 69   70   70   36

Round devices (cont'd)

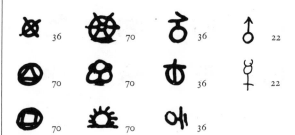

Dotted devices

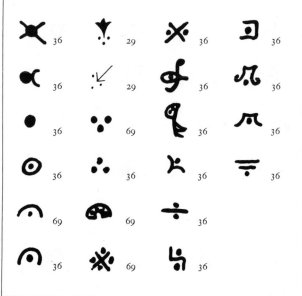

Miscellaneous devices

⬠ 69	Ŧ 36	⊬ 36	4 36
✳ 69	𝕋 36	𝕏 36	ഒ 70
✕ 69	⚓ 36	♯ 36	ൄ 69
✗ 36	↯ 36	⧺ 36	⚕ 69
卍 71	逆 36	↜ 36	ൠ 69
卍 36	⊥ 36	↑ 36	ꙮ 70
ꙮ 69	⊢ 36	↓ 70	ꭗ 71
⧻ 71	⧼ 36	⚜ 70	ꝗ 70
✢ 36	⤬ 36	↔→ 36	ꙭ 69
⊤ 36	卐 36	ψ 36	⤫ 69
𝕋 36	Ⱶ 36	⚘ 36	ꝭ 36

Miscellaneous devices (cont'd)

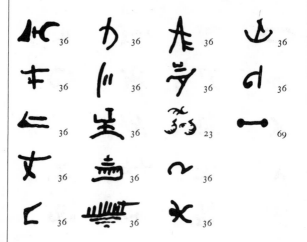